Prologue

This book, _Doctor Stories_, is the story of my professional life. These memoirs can be summed up as follows:

My career as a physician-surgeon was mostly based on anecdotal experience learned by practical observations during the initial office visit, operating room, and postoperative period; my clinical laboratory.

The most important lesson for me was taught by Ambroise Pare, father of modern surgery (1510-1590); "All doctors should remember that we treat but it is God who heals".

Table of Contents:

Chapter 1: The Making of a Doctor

Chapter 2: Medical School

Chapter 3: Residency

Chapter 4: Military Doctor

Chapter 5: Academics

Chapter 6: Medical Students

Chapter 1

The Making of a Doctor

1) In the Beginning

Importance of a College Education

My maternal grandmother, Leah Ehrlich, was prophetic in her advice. I was only eight years old when she told me in broken English mixed with Yiddish "If you want to be a "Balagoula" (wagon driver) carry a ball, but if you want to be a "Chachum" (respected wise scholar) carry a book."

In 1953, I was 17 and a senior in high school on the verge of graduation. "Enough school", I remarked. "It's time for me to go out into the world and be like my dad, a traveling salesman. He never went to college." My mom replied, "Mark, you will go to college even if you only lean against the wall." I never understood what this meant until four years later upon graduating Dickinson College. My mom's formal education did not go beyond high school, yet she knew that a college experience was the gateway to a new world; a world of classical literature, music, art, comparative cultures, religions and the ability to share ideas with professors and students with a variety of backgrounds.

The most critical aspect of her recommendation was that a college education was an absolute requirement in becoming a doctor.

"What is so important about going to college? I would be the first to go to college from our extended family and, besides, where would we get the $1000 for the first year's tuition?" I argued.

But before I knew it, I was taking a two-day placement exam at the University of Pennsylvania Psychology Department, arranged by my mom, the little huggable lady.

Two weeks later, an official letter arrived with the results. The test results indicated that I had a strong aptitude in science and was most suitable for pursuing a medical career. Wow, I thought. I had always wanted to be a doctor, but was convinced it was too hard, would take too long and was too expensive.

2)   Dyslexic

I managed to graduate Kindergarten without a hitch. The wooden building blocks, milk and cookies, nap time and recess were fun and games. First grade had its challenges with the ABC's and simple math but, again, I made it and moved on to the Second grade. By the Third grade, things became more challenging for me. I was embarrassed to stand up before the class and read or attempt to solve a math problem. I was slow to give the answers and a poor reader. I had difficulty trying to explain the meaning of stories because words had little meaning for me. My penmanship was awful, hardly legible. Plus, as a left-hand writer, I would smear over the ink of letters I had just written.

My mom was called in to meet my teacher and was told that based on my performance, it would be best if I repeated the Third grade. My mother listened and with conviction told the teacher that her son would someday become a famous educator. At that time, educators did not recognize dyslexia. My mom figured it out. She reasoned; if I was taught by changing the standard approach to one directed to my special needs, perhaps a failing student could excel. My mom was brilliant and clearly ahead of her time.

She asked our next door neighbor, Chinky Akerman, to tutor me. The kindness extended to the Akerman family by my mom was returned at a most crucial time. My mother had purchased coal for their furnace to warm their house during the bitter cold winters and gave Chinky's father my dad's winter coat and gloves. The Akerman family did not forget these kind deeds and Chinky gladly worked with me.

Chinky was in his third year at Temple University working towards a degree in Physical Education. He was on a full scholarship for gymnastics. Somehow, he realized that I had a pictorial brain and as long as a concept could be converted into a picture, it was immediately processed, stored, and retrieved upon request. After a few weeks with Chinky, I was catching on quickly. My school teacher was informed of how best to deal with my issue.

I excelled in Geometry, mechanical drawing, Physics, Chemistry, Physiology, Anatomy, Biology and of course, gym. These were all subjects that were perfect for someone with a pictorial brain. The struggle came with language, spelling, basic math, music, or any subject that was abstract, in code, and with rules and exceptions. I had to break my teeth to get through French, Spanish, and English. For me, passing grades in language required rote memory. This reading handicap required reading a sentence multiple times until the meaning became clear. I failed to connect any logic to words, numbers, or musical notes. These abstract symbols remained in the nonsensical world, beyond my comprehension.

3)   Doctor Dershaw

The result of the placement test at the U. of Pennsylvania awakened a secret yearning that I always had from the time I was a little boy. I wanted to be like Doctor Dershaw, our family physician. He was so kind, caring and gentle.

Thinking back, I remembered times my mother would call Doctor Dershaw when my sister Libby and I had a high fever, cough and a sore throat. The front door bell would ring, the door would open and close and the doctor would be heard as he climbed the stairs to reach my mom's bedroom where my sister Libby and I were in bed, lying side by side. I could hear a thump and shuffle of a shoe dragging and it would get louder as the doctor approached. Doctor Dershaw always wore an elevated special shoe to compensate for one leg that was shorter than the other. The doctor was born with severe Kyphoscoliosis (a twisted spine). This deformity produced a small statured man with a humped back. Doctor Dershaw's face was long and narrow and his chin was pointed. His voice was high pitched but soft and soothing.

He had a routine. First, he would wash his hands in the bathroom sink that was located off to the side of the bedroom. Next, he would feel for my pulse. Then gently with his warm fingers, he would pull my lower eyelid down to check the color of the lining. After a gentle feel of my tummy, Doctor Dershaw would check my blood pressure and heart for a murmur.

We would always get the same routine exam and the same prescribed medicine; a folded paper wrapper with a white powder. This was an antibacterial medication referred to as Sulfa which was the only antimicrobial medication available from 1936 until after WWII when Penicillin came into use. As a child of 4 to 8 years of age, Sulfa was the drug of choice for all illnesses that presented with fever and was effective for streptococci (strep) infections.

If Doctor Dershaw made the diagnosis of one of the contagious childhood diseases like mumps, measles, chicken pox, scarlet fever or whooping cough, a poster was placed on the window facing the street for all to see. "This House is under Quarantine until Further Notice."

That would mean we would get ten days off of school ...great news for kids! It was bed rest, lots of fluids and horrible food that was supposed to be good for you like...a milk shake with a raw egg, rice pudding with raisins and of course lots of chicken soup. We had no choice but to remain at home and take the food torture treatment...which meant forced feeding if necessary. If we tried to sneak out of the house, we were threatened with arrest for breaking the quarantine.

In 1953, when I graduated high school, a whole lot had changed from the days of sulfa and quarantines. Now there were five different kinds of antibiotics for a variety of infections, insulin for diabetics, surgery to restore hearing and so many other amazing medical advances. These were exciting times, especially for me, after being accepted to Dickinson College. Receiving a small scholarship for swimming and a prospective job as a waiter in the Phi Epsilon Pi Fraternity house helped defray expenses. I was now a premed student and started the long journey to become a doctor.

4)   The Magic Potion

In my first year at Dickinson, I qualified for the swim team. That year, I swam freestyle in the fifty and one-hundred-meter sprint events. Swimming was not possible after the first year of college because swimming practice was every afternoon. As a premedical student, I was required to attend science labs three afternoons a week.

I was determined to get the highest grades possible after a meeting with Red Malcolm, the premed advisor. He said to me, "May, to get a Jew into medical school, your people have to get better grades than the other students." This was a reminder that there was a quota for Jews. Each medical school limited admission to only a limited percentage Jews.

After that meeting I decided it would be academics over sports. I remembered my maternal grandmother, Grandma Leah Ehrlich's advice, "Carry a ball and become a wagon driver or carry a book and become a respected scholar." I was going to achieve my life's dream and become a doctor.

At the end of the third year at Dickinson, high grades rewarded me an early admission to Medical School. I graduated tenth in my class with Honors in Biology.

The early admission took the pressure off and I tried out for the swim team again in my senior year of college. It had been two years since I swam competitively and the layoff made it almost impossible to make a comeback. The team was loaded with newly recruited powerful freestylers. I thought there would be no way I would be able to compete with the freestylers and backstroke had never been my strength.

That left only one place where I thought I might qualify: the breaststroke. This event differed from the classical butterfly where the swimmer thrusts his body forward and out of the water with a circular arm motion followed by a powerful dolphin kick. It was a new event, referred to as Conventional Breast Stroke, and performed mostly under the water. It reduced the resistance and required less strength than the butterfly event. Dickinson's number one breaststroke swimmer was Lou Sprechman, the Captain of the team, friend, and Jewish fraternity brother. Lou was a champion and earned the respect of the team. I kept all this in mind when it was time for tryouts. Lou had no worries; my best time was five seconds slower than Lou.

At this point, I had thought that even if I made the team, the issue of afternoon labs still existed. The coach had been very adamant, "If you don't practice, you don't swim." I negotiated with the coach, and told him "Coach, you are one hundred percent correct about the practice policy. You know my life's dream was to become a doctor. Those who chose the candidates for medical school were rigid, 'No lab, no doctor'. Please keep that in mind. If I can beat Sprechman, your best breast stroker, would you consider making an exception for me?" The coach paused. He must have thought that without attending practices I did not have a chance, but he still agreed. "Ok, only if you beat Lou by five seconds in every breast stroke event." Great, I thought. "Deal!"

There was a three-week mid-winter break before the next time trials. I went to the Germantown YMCA and took out a holiday college pool pass. The day I got into the pool to train, there was an impressive fellow swimming laps beside me. It turned out that he was the All Colligate Breast Stroke Champion from LaSalle College. I introduced myself to this chap and explained the situation. After three weeks under his tutelage, I was able to bring my time down to be competitive with Lou.

I returned to college and beat Lou by five seconds and made the team. But now I was left thinking about how to be able to maintain the edge without being able to practice, since practice time still coincided with lab time!

Not to be deterred, I secretly made a copy of the key to the pool. I went to bed each night at eight PM, got up at three AM and worked out alone in the dark swimming pool for two hours, Sunday through Thursday. This allowed me to maintain my form and knock off another three seconds insuring I was number one as Dickinson's best in the breast stroke event.

I broke record after record with each swim contest. Our team was undefeated and had a real chance to win our division. The coach and team members could not figure how it was possible that the "Doc" could become such a sensation without coming to practice. It was my secret. No one had ever discovered that I made a key to the pool. No one ever found out that I swam five times a week, alone in the dark without supervision or protection. If anyone would have discovered the secret, expulsion and goodbye to medical school was a certainty. That secret remained a secret to this day.

The coach called me in and demanded some explanation for my spectacular performance. My teammates suspected that I was taking steroids and there were rumors that I would have been required to submit to drug testing.

The final showdown had arrived, the day when all the teams in the league competed for the championship. My coach insisted to know what I was taking. He wanted to make sure it was legal because if caught doing something otherwise, Dickinson would have had to forfeit the championship and there would have been severe consequences.

I reassured the coach that what I was taking was completely "kosher". I confessed that I made a "magic potion" in the chemistry lab and that I had enough for each member of the team. The coach showed his excitement when I took out a bag of small corked test tubes, each the size of a cigarette. Before the Championship Swim Contest, I handed out a test tube to each of my team members. I instructed them to take a sip just before their event.

With the newly found confidence in the "magic potion" each team member took seconds off their previously recorded times! That day, Dickinson was unbeatable and we won the championship. The other teams and their coaches took notice of the little test tubes and the sip each Dickinson swimmer took before he stepped up to the starting block. The other teams registered their protest with the head judge. There was a big huddle and the remaining test tubes were gathered up to be tasted by those in the decision-making position. The potion tasted like honey and wheat germ and chemical analysis confirmed the contents as just that. The officials upheld the final results of the swim contest. Dickinson was the undisputed champion.

Everyone learned from this story.

It was only mind over matter that served as the performance enhancer. Determination, resourcefulness, and a little deception are how to win championships. Those who do not practice do not become champions.

5)   Alligator and Turtle Race

Dickinson College was famous for its law school; therefore, it was not surprising that the majority of the freshmen were pre-law students. The pre-meds were outnumbered but were not to be outsmarted.
Gambling was common between the two groups and reflected the competitiveness between the two sides.

Norm, my roommate, and I were often instigators. We once announced that on a Wednesday evening at 8 PM sharp there would be a race between a one-foot long Florida Okefenokee Swamp Alligator and a giant Australian Snapping Turtle. The race would take place right in Conway Hall, the freshmen dorm. We would release the reptilian critters at the end of the hallway and the champion would be the first to cross the finish line. The pre-law students bet on the turtle and the pre-meds placed their bets on the alligator.

The word of the great race had circulated across the entire Dickinson campus.   The time, place and rules were posted. All bets were required to be placed 15 minutes before starting time. Only dollar bets were accepted and in order to remove the taint of gambling, all winnings were to be donated to the Dean's charity fund. Mr. Dietza, the Conway Hall proctor, would hold all the money. Of course, there was no way to prevent side bets.

Norm and I were counting on the alligator to win over a meandering turtle since we knew turtles do not walk straight but tend to move in circles. We would further strengthen our position by doping the alligator.
We fed the alligator steroids in the morning and evening for three days before the race. In addition, Vitamin B1, A and E were administered a week before the race and finally, Amphetamine (a stimulant), was administered just prior to the race.

The time to race had arrived. The place was jammed and the cheering had already begun. We had to restrain our alligator; his claws were digging in and his legs were in a running mode. The pre-law students placed their turtle alongside the alligator.

The starter's gun fired and the race began. It was no contest. The turtle did not move while the alligator took off toward the finish line. The turtle handlers nudged their racer but to no avail, the turtle would not budge. The alligator had reached the half-way point while their turtle was just leaving the starting line.

The supporters for the turtle were ready to tear up their bets when the alligator stammered, stuttered, rolled over, and died. The turtle won the race by default.

The pre-law students were jubilant while the pre-meds were despondent. What had happened to our doped up supercharged alligator?

Naturally, the future docs took the one-foot long Florida Okefenokee Swamp Alligator to the laboratory and performed a postmortem examination. The findings were striking. Our alligator died of liver failure due to vitamin overdose and a massive heart attack from the effects of amphetamine over stimulation.

In an effort to fix the contest, we had killed our alligator. Only Norman and I knew about the fix and the reasons for the cause of death. If our alligator had raced to the finish line and won, the lawyers would have most likely insisted that there be an investigation.

I learned an important lesson; honesty earns trust and most importantly maintains a good name.

6)   <u>Flunked English</u>

I excelled in the science classes. I majored in Biology and received top grades in Chemistry and Physics, however, I struggled with languages. This difficulty dealing with abstract concepts like language, math and the mechanics of music would haunt me throughout my days as a student. I first noted this issue in the third grade (See story #2, Dyslexic).

I overcame this handicap to some extent by sheer effort. It affected my comprehensive reading skills and required me to read and re-read everything in order to understand the underlying meaning. For example, I was never able to appreciated poetry and literature, including the great works of Shakespeare.

I have a pictorial brain; if it cannot be visualized, it does not exist. This explains why I felt comfortable as a surgeon but was never willing to read a speech.

Language was one of the prerequisites for entry into medical school. In order to be eligible for acceptance into med school, one had to get a least a B grade in Spanish and English.
In order to pass Spanish class, the students had to read a short story in Spanish. I took a whole day reading the story repeatedly until it sounded like Spanish. The teacher realized how much of

an effort I put into this project and my effort together with my ability to memorize the vocabulary earned a B; and that was only after some pleading.

Getting a grade of B in English was more difficult. The official policy of Dickinson's English department was "the five-misspelled word rule". Five misspelled words received an automatic F for fail. There were no exceptions.

My English composition teacher was one of the most popular professors on campus. He was an accomplished writer, having published a number of adventure novels. This professor cared about his students. Before the final, he warned me about the five-misspelled word rule. He encouraged me to save the last 15 minutes before turning in the final paper in order to read it over and correct any misspellings.

The professor told me that he felt I had a special gift as a storyteller and that he would leave my paper to review last because they were so entertaining.

This was reassuring. My storytelling skills I gratefully picked up from my dad and the humorous content was influenced by my roommate, Norman, who was the funniest guy I ever met. I chose to write the story about the Alligator and Turtle Race (story #5) for the final exam.

I was certain that this story would earn a B grade and satisfy the med school requirements. The professors posted the final grades in a locked glass bulletin board located in the center of the campus. Students gathered and waited their turn to check their scores. Each student had been assigned a number; this way, grades remained confidential.

My number was 104 and listed at the bottom of the second column. Right there in front was a big fat F. All that went through my mind was "There it goes! All my dreams and hard work, all the hours of study wasted. There would be no doctor in our family." I found a bench and put my head down supported by hands that covered teary eyes. I lifted my head and stared up at the sky. Maybe the score was a mistake. Maybe my number got mixed up with someone else.

The English professor lived on campus and just around the corner. If I actually failed, I wanted the teacher to tell me this to my face. The professor lived in a small modest house. The front was red brick and trimmed with narrow blocks of sandstone set around the windows. There were three steps from the sidewalk to his red front door. I grasped the black wrought iron railing and took the first step leading up to his house. At that very moment, the front door opened and a classmate of mine, Eddie Blatstein, (name changed to protect privacy) came flying down the steps and landed on his behind in front of me.

Behind him was the professor, livid with anger. "Don't you ever try to bribe your way around here!"

I began to turn and leave the scene fearfully when the professor motioned me to come in. The professor's tone had changed and in a soothing voice he asked me to sit down. "In all my years, no one has ever attempted to bribe me for a passing grade. Don't you think that the faculty knows about this guy who drives around campus in a red convertible Ferrari? Some guys think everything is for sale, well not me!"

He seemed to calm down and said "Ok, May, now let's talk about you. Please understand it was painful to flunk you just because you cannot spell. Your paper about the Alligator and Turtle Race was among the best papers ever turned in. However, this is a writing class and not spelling class so I will speak to the chairman of the department. He is the one who established the rule and he will be the one to have to break it. Give me time to present your paper to him and I will notify you of our decision." Without a word, I left the professor's house.

The very next day a sealed envelope arrived addressed to me. A voice yelled up from the front door of the frat house, "May! There's an official letter here for you. They won't release it without your signature." I ran down the flight of stairs three steps at a time and opened the envelope. The professor was able to convince the chairman to bend the rule! I received my official grade. They gave me a 'B' in English. I was back in business!

There were a few big lessons I learned here. 1) Don't ever give up! When there is a will, there is a way. 2) One's best advocate is oneself; don't be shy to speak up. 3) Nothing beats a try but a failure. 4) Always get back up if you fall down. Everyone falls at one point, but not all get up.

Chapter 2

Medical School

7)   C.P.Bailey

In June of 1957, Time Magazine featured Charles P. Bailey with his picture on the cover. He was considered the Father of External Cardiac Surgery. Dr. Bailey was the Chief of Thoracic Surgery at Hahnemann and was the author of the classic text, Surgery of the Heart. Bailey was the first to perform a Mitral Commissurotomy which was his greatest contribution.

I decided to become a cardiac surgeon and Bailey was to be my mentor. I chose Hahnemann for medical school over the University of Pennsylvania largely because of him.
The anatomy and physiology of the heart fascinated me. I had already spent three years of heart research while majoring in biology at Dickinson College. The study was in collaboration with Dr. Elmer Herber, the chairman of the Biology Department at Dickinson and Professor Myron Halpern, from the Anatomy Department at Hahnemann. Our study of the development of the coronary arteries was published in the Proceedings of the Pennsylvania Academy of Science in 1957. This was my first publication in a scientific journal.

I had to figure out how to get close with Bailey. As program chairman of our medical school fraternity, it occurred to me to invite Bailey as our guest speaker. One doesn't just pick up a phone and say "Hi" to Charles P. Bailey. I was told I needed to contact his PR person. Unfortunately, that did not get the desired response. There was a member of my medical fraternity, who was Bailey's classmate at Hahnemann and he made the contact. Bailey accepted our invitation and as program chairman I arranged to chauffeur him to the meeting.

That evening, we were all impressed with Bailey's spell binding presentation. He related how he devised surgical approaches for common cardiac problems. In the 1950's, heart disease accounted for 39 percent of all deaths. One of the most common acquired disorders was mitral valve stenosis that was caused by A. beta Hemolytic Streptococcus (ABHS). It presented with a sore throat and fever. In the 50's and prior, there was no way to differentiate between viral pharyngitis and Strep throat. Today, a Strep kit is used to diagnose the cause of the pharyngitis. Penicillin, the curative antibiotic was not available for civilian use until 1946, after WW II. As a result, Strep went undiagnosed and untreated. The complications of rheumatic fever contracted during childhood, presented in adulthood with bacterial vegetations and scaring of one or more of the four heart valves. In advanced cases, the heart was unable to pump blood past this obstruction and patients died from heart failure.

Bailey was aware that without a way to stop the blood flow and the heartbeat, surgical approaches to internal cardiac disorders were limited. Bailey's dream of a heart lung by-pass machine wasn't yet available. He was determined to be the first to surgically relieve the threat of death for patients with Mitral Stenosis. He devised an ingenious approach that revolutionized cardiac surgery and saved 1000's of lives.

He reasoned, if one can't see, then look with your finger, let touch be your sight. He described how he trained his fingers to recognize by feel all of the internal structures of the heart in both normal and pathologic states.

Bailey devised a scalpel that attached to his right index finger. This blade could be advanced beyond the tip of his finger to cut open the stenosed valve and then retracted once the procedure was completed. The blood flow was controlled by a purse string suture pulled tightly around his finger.

Now that he worked out the technique, he presented his idea to his medical colleagues at Hahnemann offering a surgical option for patients that would otherwise die. Bailey was referred patients who were near death and he operated on four consecutive referrals. None of them survived the rigors of surgery. Bailey related this period as the worse ordeal of his life. He was accused of murder performing experimental surgery. The Pennsylvania State Medical Board considered censoring him, cancelling his license to practice medicine and even criminal charges of murder. Pressure was placed on the Hahnemann Board of trustees to suspend his privileges. Before any action was taken, the fifth operated patient recovered following the mitral commissurotomy. This procedure and outcome made the medical annals. Bailey was vindicated. That night with Bailey reinforced my desire to pursue the field of cardiac surgery. On the way home, we chatted about how much I wanted to be like him. He seemed interested in the research I had completed to date and offered me an opportunity to be on his service as a medical student observer.

One session with Bailey convinced me that the life of a cardiac surgeon was not for me. I was a first-year med student and after a day in the anatomy lab, I joined Bailey and his team in the OR dressing room. Bailey and his team of Brazilian super-surgeons had just finished a long tedious procedure closing an atrial septal defect (ASD) using the donut technique. The inside wall of the right atrium was sutured to the hole between the right and left atria.

They barely had time to change out of their bloody gowns when they were called back to the OR; the patient was hemorrhaging from the chest wound. They went back and stopped the bleeding and transfused another two bottles of whole blood. I learned that this was a common event and sometimes required three go backs to the OR before the procedure was completed. The mortality for cardiac surgery in the 50s and 60s was significant; 50 percent of the patients died either on the OR table or the recovery room. This high rate of death and dying among cardiac surgery patients greatly dampened my enthusiasm to pursue this field of specialty.

Bailey was known to sleep on the OR table to ensure that he was ready to start again the following morning. One of the Brazilian super-surgeons was required to sleep in the on- call room just steps away from the intensive care unit (ICU) and OR. As part of my assignment as a medical student observer, I was required to spend a block of 24 hours with a post-op patient. I spent this time under the supervision of an on call Brazilian surgeon, Santiago. He was scheduled to take call but traded places with his colleague, Mateo. That night, Santigo's wife went into labor and gave birth to a boy.

On this particular shift, things were quiet and I got to sleep through the night. In the morning, at 6 AM, we would meet for rounds of the post-op patients, most of who were in the ICU. Following rounds we met in the OR doctors' lounge to discuss today's surgical patient.

That morning Santiago was beaming with pride and offered all of us a Cuban cigar. He knew Bailey loved to smoke a cigar, especially a Cuban which was a real treat. Bailey, moistened his cigar with his slightly extended tongue and then lit up his smoker by twirling it to be sure it was evenly lit. He took a drag and let the smoke out slowly savoring this special treat. Bailey looked up at Santiago and said to him "You know the rules. The man on call is on call and no substitutions. Clean out your locker, you're through." We were all shocked. I will never forget this moment.

Bailey was brilliant and his accomplishments put Hahnemann on the map; his bold and risk taking moves saved thousands of lives. However, this experience with Bailey and the Brazilian surgeon dampened my desire to be a cardiac surgeon.
In 1959, Bailey left Hahnemann after a dispute with the administration and relocated at Devorah Hospital in NJ. He was the first to perform open heart surgery at Devorah Hospital.
In the 50's, Bailey earned a law degree from Fordham University and in the 70's, he left his surgical practice and opened a law practice specializing in Medical Malpractice. Bailey continued practicing law until weeks before his death at age 82.

8)   <u>Dan Downing</u>

In my third year at Hahnemann, we had an opportunity to take an elective. A Hahnemann senior, Frank DeRusso, adopted me. Frank graduated from Central High School three years before me. He was an "All American" high school football player. His fierceness as an inside lineman was legendary; he looked older

than his stated age with a dark heavy beard and thick gruff
voice.

Frank grew up in "Little Italy" of South Philadelphia. This blue
collar working class neighborhood was known for turf wars
between the various racial ethnic groups who lived in close
proximity separated only by a street or alleyway. Kids growing
up in that environment required physical toughness to defend
themselves and their turf. In spite of this, Frank was a gentle
kind soul and an ideal role model.

He introduced me to Dr. Daniel F. Downing, an Assistant
Professor of Pediatrics. Downing, like Bailey, was also a pioneer.
His field of expertise was interventional radiology, cardiac
catheterization.

However, Downing was much different than Bailey. Downing
was quiet mannered, modest, shy and reserved. He was a man
of few words. He was a dedicated family man and a devout
Catholic. Dr. Downing's finger tips were discolored from
nicotine stains, a sign of an addicted cigarette smoker. The tips
of his finger were further marred from radiation burns. They
were shortened and stubby. Downing refused to wear lead
covered latex gloves that shielded his hands from radiation as
he worked under the fluoroscope performing cardiac
catheterization. He claimed that the protective gloves reduced

the sensitivity required to navigate the catheter into selected vessels.

He was recognized for his diagnostic skills. Along with the patient's history, physical exam, and EKG together with the cardiac angiography, he was uncanny in drawing a picture of the most complicated congenital defects. His diagnosis was confirmed by Bailey at time of surgery or by the pathologist at the post-mortem. He was the leader in the field and a master of fluoroscopically guided cardiac catheterization.

I got to see him in action. Every Tuesday morning, there was a mortality and morbidity conference held in the main conference room. The room was set up with fixed seating arranged in a half circle with the first row reserved for faculty and the rest for the medical students and visitors.

This large room accommodated hundreds of spectators. The rows of seats extended up and back 15 rows to the rear of the auditorium. Each row sat 20 across with an isle down the middle. It was wise for students to get there late and take a seat high up in the back as far away from the professors as possible. There were two seats in the back positioned behind a post. It would be ideal if one could secure either of these two seats. This offered protection from the view of the moderator standing at the bottom. They had an uncanny ability to call on students who never had the correct answer.

This was the combined meeting of the medical and surgical departments. All the top brass was in attendance. A complicated case was presented by the chief resident that included the history, physical findings, lab results, and special tests. Data and relevant pictures were projected on a giant twenty foot screen that rolled down from the ceiling.

The intern on the cardiology service made the case presentation. A 15 year old high school student collapsed during football practice and died quite suddenly, shortly after admission.

There was a long discussion and many questions regarding the findings. As a third year med student, this case was a real "who done it". Various differential diagnostic possibilities were listed by the Department Chairmen of Medicine, Cardiology, and Surgery. Dr. Downing was asked for his opinion before the pathologist was called upon to review the autopsy findings.

Doctor Downing stood up and walked to the speaker's podium. He was handed the microphone. He paused and then said three words: "Congenital Aortic Stenosis." He then walked back and took his seat.

He was asked how he came to that conclusion. Again, he said only three words, "Murmur, Freckle and Death." It was clear Downing was playing with them.

The Pathologist described his findings and concluded that the cause of death was Congenital Aortic Stenosis (CAS).

This was typical Downing. If anyone wanted to know how he did it, they could stop by his office.

Frank and I couldn't wait to get back to Downing's office. "You want to know how I knew. Go through my charts and pick out all the cases you can find that have Congenital Aortic Stenosis." That would be our project over the next ten months. We found 100 patients with surgical or pathologic confirmation of the diagnosis. There were no computers so all the data retrieved from our chart review was listed on extra- large sheets of paper. We studied the incidence of age, gender, physical findings, and EKG results.

When we were finished reviewing our results, we were amazed by our findings. CAS could be diagnosed by a routine physical exam performed in the office.

This disorder was more common in males; the left chest wall may be more prominent than the right because of left ventricular hypertrophy (enlargement) due to the extra work required to pump blood passed the narrowed aortic valve. The turbulence created as the blood passes through the narrow valve leading out to the neck explains why the heart murmur is heard most pronounced in the neck. There was one other discovery that was found in the majority of patients. A freckle was prominent on the skin located in the upper chest area.

These findings supported Downing's astute diagnosis. The reason he couldn't elaborate at the conference was his diagnosis was based on his impressions without hard data to support his conclusion. This paper based on Downing's work turned out to be a classic. An early diagnosis by a routine physical examination can prevent sudden death and early surgical correction can be life saving.

The paper was submitted to the Minnesota State Medical Society for their annual national contest. Papers were submitted by medical students nationwide: our paper won first prize and was published in the Minnesota Journal of Medicine, 1961.

Doctor Downing refused to place his name on the paper. This was part of his humble makeup refusing to take credit for his own work. He was the most knowledgeable and modest teacher I ever encountered; one to emulate.

Downing continued to work in tandem with Bailey at Hahnemann until the late 50s. The Director and Board of Trustees at the Devorah Hospital in NJ recruited Bailey and Downing because of their reputation for clinical excellence. They were offered a significant increase in salary, research space and financial support.

Frank went on to marry his high school sweetheart and became a successful cardiothoracic surgeon in Philadelphia.

9)   The Needle and the Brain Tumor

Medical students are like butterflies; they go through a metamorphosis. They start out the first year with long white lab coats that are worn in the cadaver dissection lab. In their second year and through graduation, the uniform changes to a short white coat. In the third year, along with the short white coat, they carry a black doctor's bag containing a tuning fork to check vibratory senses, a hammer for reflex responses, a safety pin to evaluate two- point discrimination and pain sensation, and an ophthalmoscope and an otoscope to examine the eyes and ears respectively.

I remember in med school we had a choice of purchasing our ophthalmoscope-otoscope combination from the AO or a Welsh Allen company representative; both products were comparable in price and performance. The Welsh Allen representative who made his sales pitch last was most convincing. The clincher for most of us, who took the subway to and from school each day, chose the Welsh Allen because of the guarantee. The Welsh Allen salesman offered to replace, free of charge, any Otoscope or ophthalmoscope that became damaged with no questions asked, even if the product was run over by a subway train. As far as I recall, this never happened.

The huge ego booster for third year med students was wearing a stethoscope draped around our neck. We were ready to be turned loose on the newly admitted patients. Our assignment was to make a diagnosis based upon performing a history and physical examination.

My first patient was admitted to room 1506, located on the top floor of Hahnemann Hospital. My heart pounded from the physical exertion as I raced up 15 flights of stairs in an effort to get to the patient before the resident or attending. For me, the challenge was to evaluate the patient first, make a diagnosis without being influenced by findings of the senior doctors.

You might be wondering why I didn't take an elevator, rather opted for the stairs. Part of the metamorphosis process to change a medical student into a doctor involved the emotional aspect. We were constantly reminded that we were not real doctors but a bunch of pretenders. We had no rights to reasonable working hours, no regard for limited sleep, and certainly no right to ride the elevator. We were often referred to as 'Doctor' in the most degrading tone. We were treated as pariahs, replaceable, and general nonentities, pushed aside; get out of the way or get run over. The system expected the medical student to keep a low profile. We were supposed to just do our job and no more. We all wore a pin just above our left jacket pocket. My pin said "Mark May Medical Student" as a reminder to all that I was not a real doctor.

I arrived to the 15th floor nurses' station and grabbed the chart from the rack for the patient in 1506. The chart contained notes from the admission clerk. Mr. Fleming was a patient of Professor Olsen, Chief of Neurosurgery. He was scheduled for a craniotomy in the morning for a suspected brain tumor. Craniotomy was a fancy name for cracking open the skull to look for the cause of the headache.

I was relieved to discover that I was the first on the scene. The history and physical findings were classical for post- occipital myositis; painful inflammation of the neck muscles that attach to the back of the head. Mr. Fleming was an accountant requiring hours with his head tilted down to read and record information which places tremendous stress on the post occipital muscles. He had exquisite pin point tenderness when I pushed my finger over the left post-occipital area. This is the point of muscle attachment to the skull.

I would be able to confirm the diagnosis with 0.5 CC of Xylocaine injected into the point of pain. If the pain disappeared then post-occipital myositis was the diagnosis and not an intracranial tumor.

The patient sensed my excitement and insisted that I share it with him. I explained that if an injection relieved the pain then he wouldn't require brain surgery. "Do it, do it!" He exclaimed.

I retrieved a syringe, needle and bottle of Xylocaine from the nurses' station; the painful area was injected. I came back to Mr. Fleming's room after returning the materials to the nurses' station and Mr. Fleming was dressed and ready to leave the hospital. His pain was gone!

I begged him to stay until officially discharged by his doctor.

"Why? You cured me. I am out of here."

The next day, I checked my mail box as was my routine. There was an envelope containing a letter from Doctor Cameron, the Dean, inviting me to a meeting scheduled that day at one in the afternoon in the boardroom. I was certain that an accommodation was forthcoming for my brilliant diagnosis that spared a patient from brain surgery.

I walked into the boardroom. The first thing that I noted was the highly polished, long, shiny mahogany table that filled the room. Each of the department chairmen were sitting around the table. There was the Professor of Surgery John Howard, Professor of Medicine John Moyer, Professor of Neurosurgery Nels Olsen, Professor of Pharmacology and previous Dean Joseph DiPalma, Professor of Cardiology William Likoff, and three other prominent faculty members. Dean Cameron sat at the head of the table farthest from me.

Wow, I thought, this is a big deal. I am in for a major award. Then it began.

The Dean led the discussion. In a serious tone, "Do you know what you did? You are not a doctor but only a medical student."

Suddenly, I realized there would be no reward that day but rather a lynching mob. This was the end of my promising career. All the hard work to this point wasted. My vision became blurred and my hearing dulled. In this situation, one feels as if punched in the stomach and a sense of nausea becomes over whelming and breathing labored.

Olsen, the Professor of Neurosurgery who was Mr. Fleming's surgeon quickly added, "You broke the law young man! You practiced without a license. Do you realize that the patient signed out of the hospital; his scheduled surgery was cancelled. Suppose, the patient had a brain tumor! Suppose the patient died!"

Then, the Chairman of Pediatrics saved the day. "Yes, but his diagnosis was correct and this young man saved the patient from undergoing unnecessary brain surgery."

They all agreed to reprimand me and put me on probation. My career was almost destroyed by a needle. Fortunately, in this case I was correct.

Important lessons were learned. Always respect the position of the attending physician. Never share your opinion with a patient unless you are the primary doctor. Finally, the most important lesson that I will never forget; a medical student is a medical student and not a real doctor. I had a long way to go.

10)   Kitchen Myringotomy

This is a true story except the names have been changed.

In my senior year, I was married and living off of my wife's modest annual salary of $3900 as a first year primary school teacher. An opportunity to supplement our income was welcomed. The chief of ENT, Dr. Herbert, learned that I had chosen ENT as a specialty and singled me out to take his night calls. He offered to pay me 50 dollars for one night. Great offer! I quickly accepted.

Dr. Herbert, as I recall, was tall, with meticulously groomed silver white hair. He was always dressed in an expensive custom made suit with matching socks and necktie. His practice catered to the "hoity toity" or mainline crowd who lived in large gated houses with pools in the back and butlers to open the front door.

I will never forget my first house call. "This is Mr. Wilbert Whitefield III and we are Herbert's patients. Our four year old son hasn't slept in two days and frankly nor have we. He is prone to ear infections. Would it be possible for you to make a house call?"

After being given the address and directions, I was on my way to my first house call. The Whitefield's lived in Chestnut Hill in a large colonial Pennsylvania stone home. The large gate at the entrance opened for me after I pushed the buzzer and announced myself.

I remember the driveway to the front of their house. The road to the house passed through a forested area that opened up into a large round circle. There was a fancy flowing water fountain lit up in the center of the circle and two expensive foreign cars parked on the side. One was a flashy convertible sports car and the other a sedan.

As I pulled up in my black two-door Ford Falcon, the butler opened the front door and welcomed me in. The mansion was impressive in its size and furnishings. Mr. Whitefield greeted me with a handshake. "We are delighted you could come."

I could hear the little guy's high pitched screams. He was feverish and pulling on his right ear. I was told he had a runny nose for a week and symptoms of an upper respiratory infection (URI). Often, when a child has a URI, the adenoids (a spongy gland behind the nose) swells and blocks the Eustachian tubes (ET). These tubes aerate and drain mucus normally produced in the middle ear. A URI causes the tubes to swell and become blocked and then the mucus backs up and becomes infected. The pus fills the middle ear space and causes the ear drum to bulge out. The bulging ear drum causes immense pain. If left untreated, the excruciating pain will persist until the ear drum spontaneously ruptures. Otitis Media, an infected middle ear, can lead to septicemia, a blood stream infection or meningitis, an infection around the brain.

We decided the best place to do the examination was in the kitchen where the light was brightest. There was also a large marble island in the middle of the kitchen where the youngster could be restrained. Sure enough, the right ear drum was cherry red and bulging out at me as noted through my Welsh Allen Otoscope.

I shared my findings with the anxious father and offered the options. I explained to him that we can wrap him up in a blanket and take him to Hahnemann's ER (which I hoped he would choose as he could be treated by a real doctor) or we can open the bulging ear drum right here on the kitchen table. I was in a cold sweat, praying that he would choose the first option. I didn't have the courage to tell Mr. Whitefield that I was not a real doctor and have never performed a myringotomy. However, I had watched Dr. Herb Kean, an ENT doctor, perform a myringotomy and it didn't seem so difficult.

However, the Board Room Inquisition I experienced was playing in the back of my mind (Story # 9). I made an effort to reach Dr. Herbert to no avail. Mr. Whitefield explained that he didn't want to subject his son to the "war zone" conditions of Hahnemann's ER. I informed Mr. Whitefield that I was actually a senior medical student covering for Dr. Herbert and I have never actually performed a myringotomy.

He asked, "Can you do it?" "Yes", I replied. "Then let's do it."

The father restrained his son in a blanket while I removed my myringotomy set from my doctor's bag. There was a lancet designed for performing the procedure. I placed the lancet into the opening of the black plastic micro-funnel referred to as an ear speculum. I braced my fingers against the child's head so in the event that he moved; the knife position would be maintained. Slowly the knife was advanced towards the middle ear. The procedure was totally blind and depended completely on feel. I remembered C.P. Bailey's words."If one can't see, then look with your finger, let touch be your sight." (Story # 7, Bailey)

There was a sudden release of pus under pressure that ran out of the speculum. The child's screaming stopped and he fell fast asleep. Now the toughest part of the house call kicked in, "How much do we owe you, Doctor?" I had no idea how to answer that question since this was my very first fee for service act. Professionally I quickly replied, "Doctor Herbert will contact you. Have a good evening."

11)   Cocaine Clinic

This is a true story except the names have been changed.

I was on a high after my first house call. Dr. Herbert loved me after all the praise from Mr. Whitefield. He pulled me aside, "Do you want to earn 50 dollars for another hour's work?" "That would be great."

Herbert told me that he had a stuffy nose clinic in northwest Germantown, not far from where I lived. He drove me to work the first time to show me the way. He owned an expensive car. It was in a class well beyond my Falcon. The seats were covered with soft tan leather, the doors closed with a thud, and the dashboard looked like one would see in the cockpit of a 747. Driving in the front seat of this dream car there was absolute silence except for the classical music produced by the sound system which was impressive.

We arrived at Herbert's clinic and he explained my job. He instructed me to take a strip of cotton in a bayonet forceps, dip it into the blue colored rose water solution, squeeze out the excess fluid and then slide a strip into each side of the patient's nose. The same would be done, one by one, to each of the ten patients sitting in small cubicles that were lined up next to each other. Once this task was completed, I was to go back and remove the cotton strips that were previously inserted. He left me and returned an hour later to take me home.

The following week I returned to the clinic. Most of the patients were returnees. I noticed that the patients were anxious and jittery before the stuffy nose treatment and twenty minutes later when I removed the cotton strips they were definitely mellow.

This fourth year medical student became suspicious. I asked the nurse, "What was in the blue solution?" Without hesitation, she told me, "Cocaine." That night was my last night working for Herbert and especially his "cocaine clinic".

12)   The Man in the Basement

My decision to become an Otolaryngologist was greatly influenced by the "Man in the Basement". I was a senior and on a six week clinical rotation at Harrisburg General Hospital where medical students were treated as real doctors. This was a welcomed departure from the hostile milieu at Hahnemann. The attending staff enjoyed having us. The teaching environment was very exciting and for the first time, really fun! There were no ancillary personnel like interns or residents. The medical students were appreciated because we performed the scut work and provided free labor. Our chores included admission evaluations, drawing blood for lab tests, pushing patients in a wheelchair to the radiology department, caring for the patients' daily needs, and keeping the chart records updated with the most current status and lab results. The attending staff was most grateful for our taking night call. As far as we were concerned, it was a dream; being a real doctor at last, even if it was a fantasy. After these six weeks of paradise, we would return to Hahnemann for our return to reality.

While serving at Harrisburg General Hospital, one case really stood out. A patient was admitted to the medical service to find the cause for his weight loss. He was a 61 year old and weight loss suggests a list of differential diagnostic possibilities; high on the list was cancer.

The patient completed a thorough medical evaluation. All tests and procedures performed failed to reveal a cause for his weight loss. He was in the hospital for almost two weeks and the attending physicians were baffled. It was apparent to me that the patient was hungry.

There was one other finding that was neglected as a possible cause. Maybe he had difficulty eating because he was toothless. He told me that he had dentures but they didn't fit. The patient had a large irregular mass growing down from his hard palate. This mass made it impossible for the patient to wear his dentures and even without them in, the mass itself interfered with swallowing and chewing.

This finding was discussed with the attending who hadn't noticed the mass. After it was called to his attention, he still wasn't impressed and suggested that the "Man in the Basement" take a look.

I inquired about this "Man in the Basement" and was told that he had a clinic every Wednesday at one in the afternoon. When I got to the basement with my patient, I saw The Man. He was a young guy dressed casually with jeans and fancy cowboy boots with pointed tips and elevated heals.

The basement clinic was not impressive. Thirty patients sat on benches lining each side of the narrow basement corridor. The clinic was barely illuminated by a row of exposed ceiling bulbs. "The Man in the Basement" was the ENT consultant. We were never officially introduced, so I still only refer to him as the Man in the Basement. He was amazing. He and his nurse evaluated, diagnosed and prescribed treatment for these thirty patients in less than an hour.

The ENT doc was on his way out the door when I asked him, "Can you please take a look at this growth in the mouth of my patient? "

He took a quick look with the aid of a small pocket light and responded, "Torus Tubaris, a benign Exostosis." It could be the cause of weight loss. Refer him to my office. I will remove the bony mass located in the center of his hard palate and then we will know whether this is the cause of the weight loss." We followed the advice of the "Man in the Basement". The mass was removed, the dentures were restored and the weight loss problem was resolved.

ENT was for me. Ninety percent of the time, the ENT problem can be diagnosed by looking. The most attractive part of the specialty is the opportunity to cure the patient by removing something. The choice of ENT for a specialty was clinched when I realized that if the pathology could be seen it could be photographed. Pictures are a marvelous teaching tool. The "Man in the Basement" showed me the way.

13)   Number Three

In our senior year, part of the surgery rotation involved following a patient from the Emergency Room to the Operating Room. It all started with me sitting in the library and waiting for my number to be called. There were three of us and I was number three. The drill began at 8 PM on a Friday night, the busiest night of the week for Hahnemann's ER located at Broad and Vine Streets in the center of downtown Philadelphia. It would have been preferable to be number one, get called at eight and go home to sleep by mid-night. It was the pick of the draw that this medical student would have to wait his turn.

The first two numbers were gone by eleven and now it was midnight and I hadn't even been called yet. The ER was down the hall from the library so I moseyed down to find out why I hadn't been called; maybe they did and I didn't hear my number called over the PA system; maybe I dozed off for a second. I poked my head into the ER. It was bedlam, blood and chaos, patients moaned and screamed, nurses and docs shouted orders, tubes were placed and bottles of blood hung from poles; it was a war zone.

I spotted the chief nurse, got her attention and whispered," I am number 3, did you call?"

Clearly, she was annoyed, "No number 3. Get out of the way number 3. Get back to the library and listen for your number."

I worried that in spite, she would make me wait all night for my number to be called. It seemed that my number was announced soon after returning to the library.

"Number 3 to the ER, stat!"

I grabbed my doctor's bag, slung my stethoscope around my neck and ran to the ER. The place was as I described previously. As I entered the war zone, I announced," Here is number 3." I was directed to the back corner of the ER where I found an Afro-American man who appeared middle aged lying on his back unconscious. His right leg was badly injured. There was no way to take a history so I reviewed his chart. He was sitting on a fruit crate in front of a gas station and was accidentally struck by the side of a truck after a fill up. The flesh across the top of his thigh was flayed off. The underlying muscle was exposed. His mental status was in response to narcotics given to relieve his pain. I checked his pupillary response to light. I didn't know why I did this except it was the only thing I could do while he was being rolled down the hall to radiology to determine whether his leg was fractured.

I noted that both pupils responded to light but the left pupil was smaller than the right. I had no idea what this finding meant. As the radiology resident emerged to read the films, I asked him to look at the patient's pupils with me. He told me that the patient had Addie's pupil. Great, now I had to look that up. Every med student carried a pocket sized glossary and it said that Addie's pupil had no clinical significance and further, the cause was unknown. Never the less, notation of this finding indicated that number 3 had good observation skills.

The patient was taken to the OR located on the second floor of the hospital. I was told to change into scrubs and meet in the OR. This was all new to me. I had never been in an OR. I found the OR by climbing up the back stairwell. The door was locked and the sign read Do Not Enter. I banged on the window that looked into the OR corridor when I saw an orderly walk by. He showed me where to change and instructed me to scrub up before entering the OR.

The OR was absolutely sterile. To ensure the sterility, personnel were required to put on shoe covers, wear a hooded hat with a plastic window in front of our eyes and mouth. I resembled a bee keeper in that outfit, standing in front of the scrub sink. There was a sign above the sink listing the steps required to clean. First, any debris lodged under the nails was cleared with a short pointed wooden stick. The instruction sign showed a picture of a nurse reaching above her elbows with her hands held high to prevent water from running down onto the cleaned area. This process was performed with a stiff brush and for a minimum of three minutes. The brush had hard bristles that felt like Brillo used for cleaning pots. My skin was red and raw at the completion of this process. If I had to repeat this process, a skin graft might have been required.

The circulating nurse poked her head out from the OR, "Hurry up number 3, the surgeon is waiting for you."

This Bee Man outfit wasn't working for me; every time I exhaled the plastic mask fogged up. To clear it, I had to inhale. I backed into the swinging door that opened into the OR just like I saw in movies. I turned around and a nurse dried my hands and then gown and gloved me. As I reached into the glove, my mask fogged up and I missed the hole where my fingers were to enter the glove. The glove tore and I contaminated the nurse as well as myself.

The nurse and I scrubbed again. In the meantime, the surgeon was yelling "Where is number 3?" Finally, I stood across from the surgeon trying my best to keep my plastic face plate from fogging. The surgeon was debriding the wound and in the process exposed a large vessel. Blood spurted and the surgeon asked for a clamp. Just then, my mask fogged up again and my clamp missed the vessel and clamped the surgeon's finger. Yeeeoouuwl!" he screamed. "Are you crazy number 3! You are out of here, out, out, out!" I got thrown out of the OR on my first try.

The only thing that saved me from flunking this exercise was the laughs when the story was retold. The Addie's pupil notation helped some. This was the beginning of my surgical career; not a great start.

Internship

In June of 1961, I graduated from Hahnemann as one of the top students, and was awarded membership to AOA, an honorary academic organization.

After receiving my medical degree, I couldn't wait to add MD to my license plate. I remember my Dad; he was so proud of his son, the doctor. His dream was to sit in his son's office and "kvell", a Yiddish word for experiencing ecstasy. My dad never had that moment. I opened my private practice office in January 1981 but my father passed away three months earlier.

14)   War Zone

My medical career continued at Hahnemann. I chose Hahnemann for a rotating internship. This was not the best paying job but a medical school based academic experience. I felt at home at Hahnemann.
The rotations included three months each of Medicine, Surgery and the ER. The rest of the remaining time was open for electives. I chose the ER for my elective affording me six months in the "war zone". I knew that in Hahnemann's ER there was excitement, constant life and death decisions and new challenges on a daily basis. Perhaps the main incentive to remain at Hahnemann was that I knew my teachers were close

by to consult with any problem I might have encountered; this subconscious comfort is referred to the Umbilical Cord Syndrome.

On the first day on ER duty, we got a call that a trauma case was coming in. A window washer fell off of his scaffold and fell from the 5th floor to the cement sidewalk and was barely alive. The ambulance with the pulsating screeching siren and flashing blue and red lights pulled into the driveway next to the ER. Almost immediately, this trauma victim was beside me lying on a gurney.

I was taught to step back and get an overview before diving into treating the obvious. This patient had a crushed skull with brain tissue exposed, blood oozing out of his nose and mouth, labored breathing and signs of a flail chest from rib cage fractures. ABC ran through my head, Airway, Bleeding and Cardiac function. This patient required attention to all three ABC's at the same time. To save his life would require a team effort. My first reaction was to pick up the phone and call a doctor. I was a med student a short time ago but now I was the doctor.

The head nurse recognized that I was floundering. She gently directed my hand away from the phone and said, "Lines." She guided me through the life saving measures. She handed me a large bore needle attached to a tube connected to a bottle of saline, and another such set up for the other arm. Then, a trans-oral-tracheal intubation followed. In these cases of mass trauma, the rule is every orifice must have a tube. A urinary catheter was essential to monitor kidney function and especially output.

Now the airway and circulatory needs were covered. A Nasogastric tube was inserted to determine the amount of swallowed blood and to empty the gastric contents to prevent overflow of acidic gastric fluids into the lungs. Blood was drawn to go to the lab to determine the blood count. It was also used for cross match and blood type in anticipation that blood replacement would be required. The nurse guided moves are referred to as stabilizing procedures. Monitoring procedures followed: EKG, BP and O_2 machines that were hooked up to a recording device.

By the time the rest of the team arrived, "Number 3" had things under control, thanks to the head nurse. This first experience in the "war zone" taught me the importance of the nurse.

The chest surgeon inserted tubes into both chest cavities to re-inflate the lungs and to drain accumulated blood. The neurosurgeon covered the exposed brain with sterile gauze saturated with saline and antibiotics. The general surgeon tapped the abdominal cavity for blood. This patient miraculously survived mainly because of prompt care by an expert team of trauma specialists.

In the "war zone" there were triumphs as well as disasters. A 4-year-old was brought into the ER after rescued from a house fire. His legs had second and third degree burns and his overalls were imbedded into his flesh. My job was debridement, separating his clothes from the burn wound. He was worn out from pain but continued to whimper. It got to me and I ordered Dilaudid, a low dose of 0.5 mgs (the adult dose is 2 mgs). The dose that I ordered was one forth the adult dose. I didn't know that Demerol was the preferred narcotic to relieve acute pain. The adult dose for Demerol was 100 mg compared to 2mg for Dilaudid. Dilaudid was fifty times more potent than Demerol and a respiratory depressant.

The little guy stopped whimpering as I proceeded to work on his burned leg. I looked up and noticed the resident was intubating my patient; he had stopped breathing. I was so focused on picking out the clothing remnant from the burn wound, I wasn't aware his breathing had stopped! "What happened"?! The ER resident quietly responded," I just saved your patient's life."The resident gently rebuked me for the choice of Dilaudid for pediatric patients, "You almost killed this kid."

I learned so much from this case; check conversion tables before administering medications for children. One must keep an eye on the color of the skin; dark is a sign of trouble. One must also listen for breathing and heartbeat; both are essential.

15)   <u>The King of the Gypsies</u>

There was a large tribe of gypsies that lived near Hahnemann Hospital. They came to the ER from time to time for their medical needs. One specific night, the ER was swamped with gypsies. The king of the Gypsies registered for care. His right thumb looked like it was badly infected. The thumb was red, hot, swollen and tender, the classical signs of inflammation. The findings suggested an abscess and appropriate treatment called for incision and drainage (I & D), and antibiotics.

My diagnosis was wrong; the king had gout, a metabolic disorder that deposited uric acid crystals in joints. Gout most commonly involves the big toe and not the thumb. I & D was not indicated. The proper treatment should have been medical and not surgical, a course of Colchicine and not I & D. A careful history may have revealed previous bouts of red, swollen painful joints suggesting gout. A blood test for uric acid levels would have been diagnostic.

I found that following a patient's course after treatment in the ER was invaluable. Patients were requested to return for follow-up care and if admitted to the hospital, I would visit them. This practice was crucial for my learning experience during the six months serving in the "war zone". I stepped into a crowded elevator to start my rounds. I have to admit how much enjoyment there was to ride the elevator considering just a few weeks back as a med student, I had to climb the stairs. From the back of the packed elevator I heard, "Doctor May, Doctor May!" It was the king of the Gypsies holding up his heavily bandaged thumb. He was so grateful for my care even though I knew it was wrong.

In the 60's, the fraternity of doctors was sworn to secrecy; mistakes were never revealed. Things have definitely changed since then. In Chapter 8 of this book of doctor stories will uncover the truth about medical malpractice.

16)   Box Cars in the Alley

My final story of serving in the "war zone" occurred in the alley outside the ER. Hahnemann, as stated at the outset of this chapter, is located in center city, Philadelphia. The bowery or Bums' Haven was walking distance from the ER. There, one can find a society of people who survive the bitter winters wearing rags and living in cardboard boxes. They are destitute, keeping warm with small fires fueled by methanol. This liquid is inexpensive and unfortunately toxic if imbibed. It leads to blindness, kidney failure, ataxia and loss of consciousness. Alcohol addicts in desperation, kill themselves drinking this stuff.

The police would be called to collect these poor souls and bring them to the morgue. The law dictates that these bodies be examined by a doctor to be sure they are deceased before being taken to the morgue. In one celebrated case, one of these frozen bodies was taken to the morgue. When a family member came in the morning to make an ID, the sobered up, thawed out body sat up and was very much alive!

The police knew better than to bring these frozen cadavers into the ER. Instead, the ER doc would go out into the alleyway, climb into the back of the police van and check for a heartbeat. This required the ER doc to open the dead man's jacket and shirt and place his stethoscope against filth and vermin. I developed the" no touch" technique. A dead person's pupils are dilated, making it easy to see the retina in the back of the eye ball. Box cars confirm death. Upon death, the blood flow ceases and bubbles of air form in the tiny blood vessels found in the retina. The police loved it when I was on duty. I was the fastest of all the doctors when it came to declaring, "This one is dead."

The police learned to load the body with the head toward the back door of the van. This was a great service for me; I never had to climb into the van with the body. Six months in the "war zone" gave me a jump start as a real doctor. I was no longer "number 3" and well on my way to become number one.

Chapter 3

Residency

17)   Richmond vs The Big Apple

In 1962, it was time to start my residency, one year of General Surgery and three years of ENT. The choice of ENT and a residency at MCV (Medical College of VA) was a logical decision.

ENT as a specialty was attractive to me as someone with a pictorial brain. A picture worked for me, numbers or words were abstracts that had to be converted to a picture. ENT was a visual specialty; if I couldn't see it, it didn't exist.

During this time period of my career, the Vietnam War played a key role in choosing ENT. The government offered a deferment for med school graduates, if accepted into the Berry Plan. This arrangement allowed the newly graduated doctors to finish a residency before serving two years in the military, provided the specialty was needed for the war effort. There was a shortage of ENT specialists.

Doctor Herb Kean, a Philadelphia ENT specialist whom I met serving in Hahnemann's ER, was key to my decision-making process. He highly recommended NY Eye and Ear Infirmary. Dr. Richard Belucci a famous ear surgeon was the chairman. I scheduled an interview. After waiting two hours past my interview time, Belucci appeared still wearing a bloody gown and gloves; I had guessed it was to impress me that he was a surgeon.

He was about to pass right by me, "Excuse me. I am Mark May. We had an appointment for an interview at 1 PM (two hours ago, I thought)."

"Oh yeah, May", he said with a Brooklyn accent. He sounded more like someone from a mafia movie or a NY cab driver than a department chairman. "'May...ya bin in da military?'' He asked. "No sir." I replied. All he said was "See ya laita."

It was reasonable to insist that resident candidates had satisfied their military obligation or risk being drafted right out of their residency, creating unexpected loss of staff. For me, it was Belucci's arrogance that was unacceptable.

I shared my interview experience with Herb Kean. He suggested that I apply to MCV in Richmond. He had a friend who took his residency there, and he had a rich experience caring for clinic patients. The rumor was that one would get lots of surgical experience at MCV. Most of the other residency programs involved caring for private patients and observing surgery rather than being the surgeon. This was a big plus for the MCV position.

The Chairman of ENT at MCV, Dr. Peter Pastore, was a southern gentleman contrasted to the gruff and curt Belucci. My wife, Ida Ann, pregnant with our second child, accompanied me to Richmond. Doctor Pastore was waiting for us when we arrived. He took Ida Ann gently by her arm and helped her out of our car. He was kind and soft spoken as we toured the facility.

At the end of the tour, Doctor Pastore indicated that the program at MCV would match my needs and hoped that we would accept his offer to become a member of their staff. Ida Ann and I were so impressed with Doctor Pastore that we both agreed to accept.

Year of General Surgery

18)   The Bear

I spent my first year at MCV in the General Surgery Department. My first rotation was in the Maxillofacial Surgery Division with Professor Elmer Bear. He was tall and balding and had a booming commanding voice. He was a formidable character with strong convictions. Bear was uniquely prepared to challenge the other surgical specialties as he demonstrated his skills and versatility beyond the dental realm.

Professor Bear was one of a few directors of a Maxillofacial Surgery program who was recognized nationally as a proponent for dual certification, Maxillofacial Surgery and a degree in medicine. Prior to this, a board certified Maxillofacial Surgeon depended on a medical doctor to perform a history and physical examination on all new hospital admissions.

Bear extended the boundaries of dental surgery to include blow out fractures. This injury is classically caused by a punch to the eye. The force drives the floor of the orbit down into the sinus below. Orbital trauma is traditionally managed by Ophthalmic and ENT surgeons. As can be expected, Bear's controversial ambitions were met with resistance and confrontations with ENT.

While on Bear's service, I learned how to wire teeth together and the importance of restoring occlusion in the management of patients with Mandibular Trauma. At MCV there was ample opportunity to practice; the hospital was a trauma center located off of U.S. Highway 95. In the 60s, driving cars at high speed without seat belts was a set up for the frequently occurring steering wheel trauma. Many of these victims suffered head, neck, chest and abdominal injuries.

My six months spent in the "war zone" at Hahnemann had paid off. The new residents on Bear's service were dentists and not yet MDs. They had little general surgical experience and were uncomfortable managing injuries beyond the face and jaw.

They loved having me on their team to perform a lifesaving intubation or tracheotomy to establish an airway, tap a belly to rule out bleeding and, in one case, to insert a chest tube to treat a Pneumothorax. I could read an EKG, chest x-ray and appropriately interpret lab results. They were impressed and welcomed this future ENT not realizing that soon I would be their friendly competition.

I had many experiences with Elmer Bear and ENT trauma cases. Dr. Bear instructed his residents to befriend the ER doctors and always be available when called. This policy would be rewarded by being called for facial trauma cases. They were successful until I came along, I was the night stalker. The ER doctors didn't have to call me; I was already there as the patients were brought in. I had an additional secret weapon; the ENT instructor for trauma, Wasfi Atiya, lived near the hospital and came at a moment's notice when called. Atiya was a Lebanese Christian and tough as nails. He was determined to build a trauma service.

One night, approximately two years after I started there, Bear's dental residents arrived on the scene to admit a patient with a blow- out fracture. I literally held onto the gurney until Atiya arrived. We argued that the injury involved the orbital region and was out of the realm of the dental service. Before long, Elmer Bear, the "Bear" appeared. Bear and Atiya got into it big time. They had to be restrained. We called our Chief, Dr. Pastore, the perfect gentleman. He resolved the conflict by making an agreement to alternate blow -out fractures and the dental service would treat this case. Bear won the day and Atiya was furious.

I learned a crucial lesson from Professor Bear, the importance of the three '"A"s for success.

1)   **A**vailability

2)   **A**ffability

3)   **A**bility

19)   The Hidden Cancer

My next assignment was to the Division of Head and Neck Surgery. Here was where I found my comfort zone. At MCV, the Head and Neck Surgeons dominated cancer surgery. Except for cancer of the tonsil and larynx, all cancers involving the head and neck were managed exclusively by the general surgeons. Head and Neck surgeons at MCV were trained at MD Anderson Hospital in Houston where they were indoctrinated to dominate and protect their turf from the growing ENT encroachment.

The ENT doctors mastered the art of the light bulb, the head mirror with the eye hole, and the silver stemmed small mirror used to examine the pharynx and larynx. As a consequence, the majority of patients who presented with hoarseness, difficulty swallowing, or a neck mass were referred to the ENT Clinic; the general surgeons required the ENT service for referrals.

A patient was referred from the ENT clinic with a left neck mass and a suspicious growth in the left Pyriform Sinus. The general surgical residents reexamined the patient employing direct endoscopy performed in the OR and under general anesthesia. They couldn't locate the lesion. The chief of the division was called in to consult and he couldn't find the lesion. Locating the lesion was required for biopsy confirmation to justify surgery.

They called me into the OR to check. The referring ENT resident sent a description and drawing locating the location and extent of the lesion.

I inserted the scope and took a look "There it is, in the mucosal folds in the apex of the Pyriform Sinus, a deep pocket alongside of the Larynx."

Even after I pointed out the location of the cancer, the lesion still remained obscured to the surgeons, even to the chief resident! "Do you want me to take a biopsy of the lesion?"

"Yes," doubting my claim and giving the go ahead to call my bluff.

The biopsy was read as invasive undifferentiated Epidermoid Carcinoma. They were impressed.

My reward was to be invited by the General Surgery Service to evaluate and attend the surgery as an assistant in all Head and Neck Cancer referrals. This invitation extended throughout my subsequent three years of ENT residency.

It occurred to me that if ENT could diagnose H & N Cancer then ENT should perform the surgery. It was clear to me that this field was more challenging than taking out tonsils and straightening crooked nasal septums.

20)   Green Gloves

My next rotation was with Lewis H. Bosher, a tall, lanky, personable, and accomplished Cardiothoracic Surgeon. He was one of the local good old boys, handpicked by the Board of Directors. Bosher was not only among the favored faculty members, but one of the most effective fund raisers.
While on his service, I learned how to insert a chest tube to remove air or blood. They appreciated my expertise treating patients with a nose bleed. This was common in post-op heart

surgery patients because they were anticoagulated. In the OR there were common commands during open heart surgery like raise the table, lower the table, what is the BP, serum oxygen saturation, CO_2, potassium and pH.

Bosher was in charge and easily identified by his towering figure and his green gloves. We were told that the green gloves were for Bosher's exclusive use because of a latex allergy.

The surgical procedures were tension filled. It was quite dramatic to stop a patient's heart beat and start the by-pass through the heart -lung machine. The technology had made great strides since my experience at Hahnemann with Bailey just a few years before.

Bosher never realized that I also wore green gloves, claiming a latex allergy. I tried to maintain my interest in a procedure that seemed always out of my line of sight, either the operating table was raised to the ceiling or I was pushed out of the way by a resident or fellow. This was proper because they were critical to the surgical team and I was really an observer. In order to stay in the game, so to speak, I would anticipate Bosher's rhythmic and routine requests and call out, "What is the BP, serum oxygen saturation, CO_2, potassium and pH."

I really believe that Bosher appreciated my input. Even after I left his service and for my remaining years at MCV, Bosher insisted that the ENT guy, May, be called to treat his patients with nose bleed. I was honored to serve him but insisted that the nose bleed tray included a pair of green gloves.

21)   Hail to the Chief - David Hume

I survived Bosher's service and moved on to General Surgery serving David Hume, Professor and Department Chairman. Hume was a pioneer in organ transplants and a dynamo. It seemed that he never slept and his academic office never closed. He hired three eight hour shifts of office staff to work around the clock while he often worked 24 hours without the need for sleep.

Hume was a micromanager and insisted that every patient admitted to the surgical service be presented to him on daily rounds. In spite of this, each week, the residents were able to hide a clinical puzzle from him. They would try to stump Hume at the weekly grand-rounds.

An abdominal X-ray was put up on the view box. Hume asked for a clinical history. The presenting resident responded, "No history for you."

Hume knew the diagnosis but played like they had him. Incidentally, if they did stump him, it would be the first time.

Then, Hume showed his brilliance. "No history, then there is only one thing this could be and I will provide the history."

"This teenaged student presented with belly pain. The x-ray is diagnostic of a lead pencil with an eraser that penetrated her abdominal cavity following a fall; the pencil was in the side pocket of her sweater."

The residents were flabbergasted. The chief resident couldn't contain himself. "Who told you?" Hume, with a satisfied gleam in his eye, gave his usual short answer, "If you decide to publish this as a case report, it will make the third. As a resident, I published the other two cases. "

22)   Knife in the Heart

Hume was bold, brash and determined. He rarely got on an elevator but this time as he rounded the stairs, an elevator appeared but the doors were closing. He reached between the doors and forced them open, got in and continued his journey to his office.

One night at 2 am, a man was brought to the ER with a knife wound to the heart. Hume was called as instructed. Normally, such an injury would involve Bosher and his team. Bosher was the only one who had access to the cardiothoracic instrument cabinet. It was bolted and Bosher was the only one with a key. Hume called Bosher and explained the situation. Bosher refused to avail his private instruments; they were needed for his private patient scheduled for open heart surgery in the morning.

Hume clicked the phone down and sprung into action. It seemed that Hume pulled a crow bar from his back pocket and ripped open Bosher's private stash. The heart wound was repaired and the patient survived.

Bosher's case was rescheduled.

This set up an institutional crisis. Bosher made his plea to the board of trustees; this behavior was intolerable. Bosher demanded that the Board decide, it would either be Bosher or Hume.

A compromise was reached. Hume got his own cardiothoracic instruments and agreed to leave elective Cardiothoracic Surgery to Bosher. Bosher was relieved of unscheduled emergencies admitted through the ER. These cases would be managed by Hume.

23)   Rounding Bases

Hume's bull like personality was demonstrated at his annual staff softball game and BBQ celebrated at his ranch where he raised long horn steer. He always batted first to set the tone for the game. He hit a slow grounder fielded by the third basemen. The throw was close and Hume crashed into the first baseman sending him flying into right field. The first baseman dropped the ball. Hume immediately headed for second. The scene that occurred at first base was repeated at second base. Hume rounded second and the third baseman was waiting to tag him out. Before the tag could be made, the third baseman became another victim of Hume's determination to score. Now, the catcher holding the ball with both hands, planted himself, protected the plate and waited for Hume.

Everyone watched as Hume picked up the speed of a run- away train and headed for home plate. The catcher, the chief resident, was not going to be intimidated. He held his position. The collision was impressive. Both Hume and the catcher were slammed to the ground in front of home plate. The resident was out cold and the ball rolled out of his mitt. Hume crawled to the plate and scored. After a splash of cold water, the resident regained consciousness. His pride was hurt more than his body.

24)   <u>Airplanes</u>

Hume bought an island off the coast of Florida. The only way to get there was by boat or small airplane. The boat trip was too slow for Hume, instead, he took flying lessons at the Richmond airport. A solo pilot's license required 50 hours of flying time. Hume qualified in one month.

He spotted a surgical resident leaving for home after a night on call. The resident was invited to join Hume for a ride in his airplane. When they got to the airport, Hume suggested that the resident call his wife and inform her that he is with the chief (Hume) and they would be gone overnight and back tomorrow afternoon. Hume wanted company for his maiden flight to his newly acquired island.

In 1973, ten years later, when Hume was just 55 years old and in his prime, he died in a plane crash. He rented an Aero Commander 560 and took off from the Van Nuys Airport located in the Suburbs of Los Angeles. He was flying alone. The plane lost power on take-off and crashed into the Santa Susana Mountain exploding on impact.

My experience with Hume was memorable. He was the consummate surgeon, a dedicated family man, and leader of men. He was driven to excel in all his endeavors. His life was on fast mode with no down time. He led by example, if only we mortals could keep up his pace. He was loved and respected by his team. Hume demonstrated to me that dedication and willingness to work harder than those around him was his secret to success. His superior intellect was certainly an important factor.

25) The Axe and the Bandaid

In the 60s it was normal for a resident to report to duty at 6 am and work 72 hours, get 12 hours rest and report back again for a 72-hour shift.

Some services were busier than others. Neurosurgery was known for almost zero sleep and the calls were constant. I was a first year rotating surgical resident at MCV assigned to the neurosurgery service.

Normally there were two of us on duty. The junior resident was on active call and the chief resident was available for backup. On this particular shift, the chief resident was not to be called unless the patient required surgery since he had a personal problem at home.

The on-call room was a small and windowless. It was only large enough to accommodate a cot, bed stand, lamp, desk, chair and wall phone that could be reached while lying down on the cot.

Back then, there were no cell phones or beepers. The doctor was alerted by hearing his name paged over the hospital PA (public address) system or directly by ringing the phone in his on-call room.

After two and a half days with very little sleep, I became like an addict willing to say anything to satisfy the need for sleep. I was struggling to keep my eyes open. I collapsed on the cot with my shoes and clothes on, feeling as if I had passed out. The phone rang. With my eyes still closed, I answered, "What time is it?" It was the nurse on the neurosurgical floor. "Doctor, it is 3 am. Do you know Sammy?" she asked.

Sammy had survived a motorcycle accident but had suffered a severe head injury and was a frightening character. Only his eyes peered through his head dressing. Sammy was a roamer and strayed off the Neuro surgery ward into the adjoining Pediatric area. He moaned and howled and scared the "heebie jeebies" out of the children.

The nurse requested that I come and lead Sammy back to his bed. I told her that there was no need. "What do you mean?" She asked. Apparently, I told her, "Shoot him with a silver bullet." However, I have no recollection of doing so! "Are you crazy?" she exclaimed. "Not at all, look out the window. Do you see it? The moon is full." Once again, I told her to shoot Sammy with a silver bullet, which is the only way to stop the howling of a werewolf when there is a full moon. She hung up and didn't call back.

The next call came at 4 am, only two hours before my shift ended.

"This is the ER nurse calling. The police just brought in a guy with an axe in his head." Still in a deep sleep, I asked about his vital signs, such as blood pressure, state of consciousness and response to things such as his name, date and who the president of the United States was at the time. She told me that all seemed normal. I told her to order an H &H (Hemoglobin and Hematocrit) and call me back with the results. She called back an hour later saying that the results were normal. While still lying limp with eyes closed, I ordered a skull series (radiographs to determine if the axe penetrated into the intracranial compartment).

The nurse was insistent that I get out of bed and come to see the patient. "Do you realize how disturbing it is for the other patients to watch this guy walking around our ER with an axe in the middle of his head? What do you want me to do?" She asked to which I replied "OK, OK. Put a band aid on it and call me in an hour." At this point the nurse was hysterical, "Did you say put a band aid on it?"

She called me at 6 am and reported that the axe did not penetrate and there was no evidence of intracranial injury. "Now are you going to come and see this patient?" I told her it was time to contact the new man on call, my shift was officially over. At this point and out of frustration, she warned me that this case would be reported to the Chairman of Neurosurgery.

Sure enough, two days later and after I had a good night's sleep, I was called in to meet with the Chief (as he liked to be called since he was a retired naval officer). He reviewed the facts as documented by the ER nurse. "May, is this true?" "Chief, I have no recollection of any of this. It was the end of my 72 hour on call shift. My brain was in a deep sleep and yet according to the report, my responses were right on. In the morning, the axe was removed and the patient was discharged with just a band aid as I recommended." The Chief admitted that the management was remarkable considering that it was accomplished while completely sound asleep. My outrageous behavior was overlooked because I was correct.

Normally, one cannot make excuses to justify such behavior. The ER nurse was correct to expect me to get out of bed and evaluate this patient. I was a victim of the system. It is unreasonable to expect anyone (doctor, airline pilot, bus driver, etc.) to perform without the proper rest. Today, there are laws that enforce limited working hours and require proper intervals for rest. However, unlike some other professions, a surgeon must finish what is started. There are procedures that take over 8 hours to complete and stamina, focus and dedication are part of the job.

26) Vegetable Garden

Every Wednesday around noon, the Coca Cola truck pulled up to the front of the ER at E.G. Williams Hospital. The soda man replenished the Coca Cola vending machine that stood just inside the entrance to the hospital.

One day things were different. Joey, the soda man's eight-year old son, went to work with his dad and sat in the front seat on the passenger's side. As the father walked around the truck to make his delivery, Joey opened his door to join his dad. In the process tumbled out and landed on his head. The father dropped the case of soda, picked up his limp unconscious son and ran to the ER for immediate medical attention.

I was on duty and began the drill that was practiced so many times. The drill first learned as an intern in the "war zone" in Hahnemann's ER. The reader must keep in mind that this was 1962 and the approach to trauma management was primitive, compared to today's standards.

In the 60s we applied the ABC's: Airway, Bleeding and Circulation. The eight- year old convulsed, his eyes rolled back and breathing ceased. His skin color darkened and I couldn't intubate this stiff convulsing youngster. I reached for a scalpel, fixed the trachea between my two fingers, opened the trachea and inserted a tube. The airway was now secured and breathing was assisted with an attached compressible bag connected to a flow of oxygen.

It appeared that his injuries were limited to his head. Heart rate and blood pressure were in the normal range. His pupil size remained equal and responsive to light. Dilantin controlled the seizures. Plain skull radiographs showed an un-depressed skull fracture. MRI and CT scans were not available in the 60s. A spinal tap showed minimal blood and the pressure was within normal. Joey was admitted to the neurosurgery service in a deep coma.

As was my policy since days as an intern, patients under my care admitted from the ER were followed. They were visited on a daily basis. I was present on the morning of the first day after admission when the chief of neurosurgery made rounds with his staff.

The chief inquired about me when he realized that I was not part of his staff. I perked up and introduced myself as the ENT resident who performed the emergency trach in the ER. He turned to me. I was certain that he would recognize me for a job well done. Instead, he berated me in front of all present.

"Look around young man and what do you see?" It was a question that did not need an answer. The ward was filled with brain damaged patients commonly following a stroke, brain surgery or a motorcycle accident. They were all dependent on life support, a trach tube attached to a respirator, a feeding tube hooked up to a bag of liquid nourishment, a urinary catheter to monitor output and a diaper. These patients required rotation every hour to avoid pressure induced bed sores. One nurse and two aids were assigned to the ward of ten patients.

I will never forget the final words from the Chief of Neurosurgery, "May, your heroic act added one more vegetable to our garden!"

I visited Joey every afternoon during my four-month tour of duty at E. G. Williams Hospital. His condition was unchanged; he remained in a coma, unresponsive and dependent on life support since the day of admission. Joey's parents were grateful that he was alive and prayed that one day he would open his eyes and smile. They never gave up hope for their only child who they loved so much. On my last day, I explained to the parents that my prayers were with Joey and the family. They hugged me for saving their son's life.

A year passed before my second rotation at E. G. Williams Hospital. I was told that several months prior, Joey was discharged to a step-down care center for head injury patients. One day around noon as I was leaving the hospital, a Coca Cola truck pulled into the driveway in front of the ER. Joey's dad was the driver and our eyes met. As he slowly approached, he leaned out of the window and greeted me. In the passenger seat next to him was a young man. Joey's dad got out and came around to the passenger's side. He helped his passenger out of the truck cab and whispered, "Say hello to Doctor May. He saved your life." He limped over, gave me a hug and with a slurred but intelligible speech pattern thanked me for being his doctor. That was a major chill and thrill moment for me.

This was heaven's answer to the Neurosurgical chief who suggested that a doctor can choose who will live or who will die. That moment reinforced the reason I became a doctor. It is the only profession that can relieve pain and suffering as well as save and preserve life.

ENT RESIDENCY

27)   Polio Over the Phone

Upon completing a year of General Surgery, I joined Doctor
Pastore to begin three years of ENT residency. Doctor Pastore
taught me an important skill; how to make an accurate
diagnosis. This was achieved in most cases by applying the art of
history taking and performing a complete physical examination.
He would always say, "Don't stop the search with the obvious;
rather continue until you find the hidden clues."

Doctor Pastore at Mayo Clinic had trained and specialized in
treating allergic disorders. His real love was solving diagnostic
dilemmas and the Mayo Clinic ENT had its share. The
differential diagnosis of headache, nasal congestion, post nasal
drip, sinus, hearing loss, ear ringing or tinnitus, dizziness, mass
in the neck, difficulty swallowing and hoarseness make up a
partial list of disorders referred to ENT doctors. The ENT
specialist is the medical expert of disorders that involve the
head and neck. There are no other disciplines in the medical
field who routinely examine the ear, nose and throat. As a
teacher of medical students, I stressed this by showing a picture
of a patient wearing a brown paper bag over his head as the
internist takes a history.

I was requested to evaluate a patient in the ER; a teenager who had been evaluated and treated the night before with a sore throat and red swollen tonsils. He was having trouble swallowing; the liquid penicillin prescribed regurgitated out of the patient's nose with each effort to take the medicine. I was stumped so I called Pastore and related the story. Without hesitation he replied, "Immediately call the resident assigned to infectious disease and tell him that this patient has polio." The diagnosis was confirmed. This was just one of many examples of Pastore's diagnostic acumen.

In addition to the importance of making the correct diagnosis, Doctor Pastore was an addicted archivist. He insisted that, whenever possible, abnormal findings should be documented with a picture. The on-call resident was issued a camera for this purpose. Doctor Pastore was responsible for my routine picture taking of all unusual findings. When he was consulted regarding a problematic patient, Doctor Pastore would say, "Did you get a picture?" This was the origin of the adage: "If there's no picture, it never happened!"

28)   Librarian with a Crooked Smile

The librarian, a single lady in her early 30s, was well known to the ENT service. She has been a clinic patient since childhood. The problem started with recurrent drainage from her right ear.

In spite of appropriate medical treatment and five surgical procedures for mastoiditis and cholesteatoma, her ear was draining once again.

The last surgery had been performed two years prior to this visit. The ENT resident surgeon recorded that a "Rambo" procedure was done. This operative approach was designed by a New York City Otologist, named Rambo. The technique involved drilling away the mastoid cells from the bone behind the ear, connecting the middle ear to the mastoid making one large open cavity and then filling it in with muscle taken from above and behind the ear. This excavation and filling approach for recurrent mastoiditis and cholesteatoma, a benign invasive ingrowth of skin, proved ineffective in her case. This Rambo procedure is still useful to fill bone cavities following skull base surgery.

The patient was admitted and scheduled for her sixth procedure. This time it was my turn to accomplish what my predecessors failed to accomplish. I was going to remove the infected tissue, the cholesteatoma remnants, and stop the drainage. Clinic cases were scheduled at the end of the day after the private surgery schedule was completed. The clinic cases on the Otology service were performed without supervision; the attending was called on an as needed basis. Hayden preferred not to be called. His policy was that we learn by watching him operate on his private patients and then practice what we learned on clinic patients.

I felt prepared for this case after practicing drilling twenty cadaver temporal bones in the lab and observing Hayden perform mastoid surgery on multiple occasions. Drilling dry cadaver temporal bones and observing a master surgeon did not prepare me as I had hoped; it was boot camp versus real combat. This day would be my Waterloo.

The case started at 4 pm. I sat on the right side of the patient. The side of the head around the right ear was shaved; the operative area was prepped with Betadine and draped with sterile towels that were sutured in place. The operating microscope which was covered with a sterile drape was positioned and the OR table rotated away from me for maximum visualization of the operative site.

Foul putrid drainage was oozing out of a small hole behind the ear. An incision was made through the area of drainage. White smelly cheesy material squirted out of the wound. This substance was typical of cholesteatoma. The incision behind the ear was enlarged following the scar from the previous surgery. The wound was held open with a self- retaining retractor.

All the loose white cheesy excess was scooped out and the remainder was flushed out with saline. A large open cavity with diseased bone and fingerlike extensions of skin (cholesteatoma) were noted penetrating the remaining mastoid cells. No landmarks could be identified. The original boundaries and contents that I had noted in the temporal bone lab (or while observing Hayden operate) were nowhere in sight. Should I quit? I asked myself. I wanted to call Hayden, the chief of the Otology service, but that wasn't an option. Hayden made it known in strong terms to never call him at home.

I began to probe the soft bone and pick at the cholesteatoma gently using the back of a Curette, a metal micro spoon like instrument. At that moment, between the middle ear and mastoid there was a structure that looked like the facial nerve. It had a disruption or gap. Now I had to call Hayden. It was 9 pm. I hadn't even realized how much time had gone by. Clearly this was a strong sign that I was lost, over my head, and in deep trouble.

The urgent call was made. Hayden showed up at 9:30 pm and without a word spoken, grabbed me by my collar, yanked me backwards, and propelled me against the far wall. My chair hit the wall and I landed on my behind. I was thoroughly humiliated in full view of the operating room staff. This low point prompted me to consider quitting. Hayden repaired the damaged nerve, packed the wound with medicated Gelfoam, sutured the incision, and promptly left the way he entered, without a word.

The librarian survived her sixth ear operation. The wound healed and the post- operative total facial paralysis slowly recovered over a period of a year. The recovery was marred by a crooked smile; thus my patient was named, the Librarian with the Crooked Smile. This was my first experience with a patient who suffered a permanent defect for all to see caused by my misadventure. She became reclusive and withdrawn. She changed her hair style to camouflage her deformity. Now I understood the Phantom of the Opera syndrome. This case had a profound impact on the rest of my career.

My response was noted by some of the faculty who came forward to ease the pain. I was told that the risks of complications increased dramatically in re-operated patients. Every Otologic surgeon will eventually cause a facial paralysis. This particular case was a challenge for the most experienced surgeon and lack of supervision played a large part that lead to the injury. This was the start of my taking on the facial nerve as a mistress, a love affair that would last thirty-six years. Managing facial nerve disorders became an obsession. One other lesson learned that will never be forgotten; how to give rebuke.

29)   The Nature Clinic

The Night Clinic provided after hours health care for Richmond's indigent population. It was staffed by the MCV medical and surgical residents. We received 25 dollars for two hours of work. This was a good deal for me whose monthly salary was a meager 125 dollars.

Each of us had a small office with a desk and two chairs for the patients. Things were routine until an old timer in his 80s complained of problem with his nature. I immediately thought he had a problem with anger control as one would expect from someone who was mean natured. As his story unfolded it became clear what he meant. He was a lady's man and attracted a younger crowd. The poor guy just couldn't keep up with the demands; he wanted something to give his nature a boost.

At first, I had no idea how to deal with this problem. This definitely was not covered in medical school or for that matter I wasn't aware that this condition even existed. Then, I recalled that in undergraduate school, during psychology class, we improved the libido in lab rats with Vitamin E. After consulting with the night clinic pharmacist for the proper dose, I wrote the troubled old timer a prescription for Vitamin E, to take one before bedtime. This worked so well for the guy that the word got out. There were lines of male patients waiting to get a prescription for the "magic pill".

The night clinic provided a unique experience. Along with "nature patients", a whole variety of other complaints were sorted out. An 18-year-old was concerned about an unsightly scar in her lower neck. I assumed from its appearance that in the past she had thyroid surgery. The real plus working the night clinic was the availability of records. Most of the patients who came to the clinic had records dating back to the time of birth and every medical/surgical event until death. This young lady required an emergency tracheotomy following a routine tonsillectomy when she was 4 years of age. The record showed that the ENT resident surgeon who dictated the operative report was Douglas Hayden. He described difficulty controlling bleeding and prolonged surgery time, which led to tongue swelling from the pressure of the tongue retractor. This patient's record was quite insightful for me. First, I learned that Hayden was an ENT resident at MCV, 14 years prior. Second, I could commiserate with Hayden because I had a similar experience with a patient that I had operated upon.

Several months before, at the weekly morbidity and mortality (M &M) conference, I had to recount the details that lead to the need of performing a tracheotomy following a routine tonsillectomy. This is a painful experience when one is required to stand before an auditorium filled with faculty members, residents, interns, nurses and medical students.

Overall, the anticipated inquisition was positive and useful lessons were shared. There was a discussion about indications for a tonsillectomy, the pre-operative minimum tests for bleeding problems, surgical technique and management of complications. However, Hayden was not so forgiving and harsh with his criticism (See story #28). Hayden had an opportunity to admit that complications occur in the best hands and how one deals with the complication is critical. He could have even admitted that when he was a resident, 14 years ago, he had a similar experience.

Twenty- four years later, Hayden had an occasion to visit me while I was seeing patients in my private office in Pittsburgh. By this time, I had earned a place in the international ENT community as a recognized expert in the surgical management of facial nerve disorders. As one can imagine, he was still my teacher and just as intimidating. I greeted him cordially. He informed me that he was in Pittsburgh because his wife required special treatment at the U. of Pittsburgh. Then he dropped the bomb. "Mark, I always admired you and recognized your drive for excellence. I was rough on you to prod the best out of you."

After Hayden's passing, I had the honor to be invited back to MCV as the first Douglas Hayden Memorial Lecturer.

30)   Tin Horn from St. Petersburg

MCV, the University Center, would get patients transferred from St. Petersburg's General Hospital from time to time as it was only approximately 25 miles from Richmond. A four- year-old was referred from St. Petersburg's. The referring diagnosis was peritonsillar abscess. I was a first year ENT resident called to the ER. I looked into the child's mouth and there appeared to be a peritonsillar abscess pushing the left tonsil past the midline and obstructing the normal space between the tongue and palate. To me it looked like the "abscess" was bulging and ripe for draining.

This seemed like a routine case of a peritonsillar abscess. The child was taken to the OR, intubated and administered general anesthesia. The moment the bulging mass was incised, blood shot out of the wound into my face, blinding me. I instinctively stuffed his mouth with gauze to tamponade the bleeding. An estimated 200 cc of blood was lost with that initial gush.

I then switched into crisis mode. The trauma training from my six months working in the "war zone" of Hahnemann's ER, kicked in. The carotid artery was the only structure that would let loose like that. "ABC"s of life saving measures became a priority. Airway was secured and bleeding controlled. Blood was drawn and sent to lab with request for 4 units of whole blood (2000 cc).

It was evening and I was working with a limited number of OR personnel. My first rational thought was to call back up. The Chief of ENT, Doctor Pastore was on call. "Hello", it was Mrs. Pastore. She told me her husband was sick in bed with the flu, high fever and hadn't eaten much in two days. "Can I speak with him? I have a life and death situation." Pastore picked up the phone sounding weak and barely audible. I explained the situation and told him that the carotid artery blew at the moment the peritonsillar abscess was incised. "Hang on, I'll be there in 20 minutes!" He said. "Great, in the meantime the blood that was ordered would become available."

Pastore literally staggered into the OR. He looked pale. I reviewed the story and informed him that 250cc of blood had been replaced following the first bleed. He leaned over the head of the table and into the patient's mouth. "OK, let's see what we have here!" Slowly, I rolled the pack away from the left tonsil area. Then suddenly, a gush of blood spurted out into Pastore's face, completely covering his eye glasses, now blinding him. I quickly pushed the pack back into place to stop the bleeding. I looked up and Pastore was lying on the floor, unconscious. He was made comfortable and when he regained consciousness a few moments later, arrangements were made to take him home.

Another 250 cc of blood was replaced. Then a tracheotomy was performed to allow complete access to the tonsil area without hindrance from a transoral endotracheal tube. The left neck was explored and the internal carotid artery was dissected to identify the most proximal segment close to the skull base. The complete lack of branches distinguishes the internal carotid from the external carotid artery. A vascular loop was placed around the internal carotid artery and tightened to evaluate the effect on the bleeding. A cerebral circulation compromise in a child this age was unlikely to cause a stroke.

Once the proximal internal carotid was ligated, the pack was slowly rolled away from the previous site of bleeding. There was no further bleeding. The pack was replaced as a precaution. The nurses and technicians present were relieved and clearly impressed with the performance of this young surgeon. The patient was transferred to the Intensive Care Unit (ICU) with the trach tube and packing still in place.

This ordeal took 4 hours. The anxious parents were updated to the critical situation. Our plan was to leave the pack undisturbed for three days. The next evening, I was called because fresh blood was dripping from the boy's mouth. 250 cc of blood was transfused and the pack was reinforced. George

Williams, a new member of the faculty was consulted. Williams had recently completed two years of Otologic surgical fellowship, one with Schuknecht in Boston and one with Guilford in Houston. These two men were among the top Otologic surgeons in America and both were internationally acclaimed.

I reviewed the case with Dr. Williams and he explained that once the parents provided that the problem started with a tin horn injury, everything became clear. This was a classic case. The child ran and fell with a metal tipped horn in his mouth. The horn penetrated the area of the left tonsil and produced a weakness in the wall of the internal carotid. This accident led to the creation of an aneurysm, which can easily be misdiagnosed as the more common peritonsillar abscess. Over a period of a week, the young patient spit up blood on two occasions. This is referred to as sentinel bleeding, a common sign of an impending rupture of an aneurysm. The other sign to differentiate abscess from aneurysm are pulsations that are visible and palpable.

Dr. Williams explained that to stop the bleeding in this case, one must prevent back bleeding from above the aneurysm. Clearly, the ligation below the aneurysm was ineffective because it only controlled blood flow from below. Blood flow at the base of the skull is unique with cross over through the Circle of Willis.

This provides blood flow coming from the normal side to the area above the aneurysm. Today, the invasive radiologist would place a balloon into the area of injury. This was not an option in 1963.

Williams planned to stop the bleeding by approaching the aneurysm through the middle ear.

The site above the injured carotid is at the bottom of the middle ear. Williams exposed the vessel working with a binocular operating microscope and through a mini speculum, a small funnel that fits into the external ear canal. The ear drum was lifted and the middle ear was exposed. Williams used micro diamond burs driven by a mini drill used for stapes surgery. He removed the thin shell of bone over the carotid. He then used something called Surgicel, special coagulating gauze, and gently depressed the exposed carotid until completely collapsed. The packing was layered to fill the middle ear space. The ear drum was placed back into its normal position and the surgery was completed. The total operating time was one hour and without any blood loss.

The packing in the mouth was removed on the third post-operative day. There was no bleeding. As a precaution, the tracheotomy tube was removed four days later. The child was discharged without any further bleeding. There were no neurological deficits. The only reminder of his death-defying experience was the conductive hearing loss which was temporary and eventually recovered to a functional level.

"Wow," I thought. "I just witnessed a miracle". The tragedy was that this case was never reported until now. Dr. George Williams changed my life by stressing the importance of a Fellowship, particularly if I wanted to pursue a teaching career. Dr. Williams was a consummate teacher and one that I wanted to emulate. Upon Professor Peter Pastore's retirement, Doctor George Williams was appointed Chairman of the Department of Oto-Laryngology Head and Neck Surgery at the Medical College of Virginia (MCV).

31)   Run Away Tonsil Clamp

In the last year of my ENT residency, I learned that I have much more to learn. The making of a doctor goes beyond books and the classroom. The greatest lesson to learn is taught by experience. Some young doctors, after thirteen years (four years of undergraduate school as a premed, four years of med school, a year of internship and four years as a resident) believed there was nothing more to learn. I was one of "some" of the young doctors.

A six-and- a- half foot, 250-pound giant walked into the ENT clinic holding his mama's hand. His little mama did all the talking for her 25- year- old son. She made a good case for taking out her son's tonsils. This immature mama's boy drooled from the corners of his mouth and had a definite abnormal speech pattern. He sounded like he had a hot potato in the back of his mouth. This was a classical picture of enlarged tonsils. The drooling indicated that he had difficulty swallowing. My examination of his mouth revealed huge tonsils so big that they met in the midline causing obstruction. The mother added that her son had difficulty sleeping and struggled to breathe when lying down.

These findings meet the criteria to justify a tonsillectomy. "How long has your son had these problems?" "Since he was a little boy", She replied. "Why didn't he have the surgery when he was little?"

The mother told me that he was so frightened to leave her that he refused to cooperate. He only finally consented because he was having such trouble breathing. She added, "The doctors we have seen, refused to accept him as a patient because he was so big." "Now, that's strange," I thought.

Sometimes an elective tonsillectomy is not done and should be delayed until a child reaches age of four but this is the first time I ever heard that size of an adult was a contraindication for a tonsillectomy. I was curious to learn the names of the ENT doctors who turned him down and why but I never inquired. Clearly, whatever the challenge, I thought I can do it. This was my last year as resident and being chief resident, I requested that this patient be scheduled and I would perform the surgery under local anesthesia. Local anesthesia was preferred for adults. The surgery was done as an outpatient procedure with discharge the same day. This way there would be less blood loss and the use of local eliminated the risks of general anesthesia.

The patient was sedated and placed on the OR table. Temporary sides were added to accommodate his arms and legs that extended beyond the table. His wrists were restrained to discourage reaching into the operative field. The anesthesia was injected. So far so good, nothing to it, I thought. I grasped the right tonsil with an extra long clamp used for abdominal surgery. The handle extended well beyond his mouth. Then, just as I was about to make the initial incision, he mumbled, "I want my mama."

Like in a Frankenstein movie, the giant broke his restraints, sat up, jumped off the OR table and headed for the hallway. The clamp hung out of his mouth and the back of his gown was wide open exposing his behind. He was chased down by security and tackled to the ground. I ran along in pursuit, rolled him over and retrieved the tonsil clamp. He then got up and ran for the door, never to be seen again.

The surgery was a disaster yet many lessons were learned. This experience taught me to recognize an impending tsunami. When the sea recedes... get off the beach. Looking back, there were definite warning signs. This man was turned down by respected colleagues because he was too big to control under local anesthesia. In those days general anesthesia had significant risks and local anesthesia was preferred. As a general rule, if other respected colleagues find reason to reject a patient, be forewarned. Normally, a physician should be guided by what is best for the patient no matter how difficult for the doctor. This case represents an exception. This will always be remembered as "The Run-Away Tonsil Clamp."

32)   <u>West Virginia Coal Miner</u>

1966 was my last year of residency. I spent three months in charge of the ENT service at the VA (Veterans Administration Hospital) located on the outskirts of Richmond, Virginia. The campus was spread out over a huge area of real-estate, perhaps equivalent to eight football fields. This layout was in response to the cold war threats between the USSR and the USA that started in the 50s. Each threatened to launch a barrage of intercontinental missiles tipped with an A- Bomb. The U.S. government thought that some resources could be spared if the hospital was spread out over a vast area and built low to the ground.

The hospital was all on one level and separated into sections. Each specialty had its own wing except for ENT. Our patients were dispersed and found in General Surgery, Internal Medicine, or whichever service they had been admitted to. Our quarters, the on-call room, was located at the extreme other end of the hospital complex and took 20 minutes jogging to answer a call. To address this problem, the on- call residents were assigned a golf cart that allowed them to cover this expansive hospital campus.

One of the patients that I was asked to evaluate was on the General Surgery, Head and Neck service. Mr. Gray was a tall well-built coal miner from West Virginia. His main complaint was hoarseness and some minimal stridor or breathing restriction. These symptoms were present and becoming worse over several months. A mirror exam of the larynx was difficult because he was a gagger. A proper examination was carried out in the OR under general anesthesia. Inflamed pebble looking structures were noted on his vocal cords, something I had never seen before.

The biopsy report solved the mystery. This West Virginia coal miner had a fungal growth on his vocal cords. The VA pathologist arrived at the diagnosis of Coccidioidmycosis after consulting with Doctor Vincent Hyams, Chief of the United

States Institute of Pathology. Doctor Hyams was the world's leading Head and Neck Pathologist.

Amphotericin B, a new antifungal agent became available in 1959. The drug was efficacious but carried a significant risk of kidney toxicity and deafness.

At that time, I was doing research with ultra sound and treating juvenile laryngeal papillomatosis, a common benign tumor involving the vocal cords of children. I was granted permission by my superiors to apply ultra sound to the fungal condition. After the risks, options and benefits were explained to the patient and he gave permission, treatment was started. The ultra sound machine was portable and treatment was administered by the bedside. After the third treatment, the fungal involvement seemed to be resolving. We were all hopeful of a favorable outcome avoiding the risks of Amphotericin.

It was decided to wait a few days to determine the full effect of the treatment. On the third day, I received a frantic call from the head nurse of the General Surgery Head and Neck Ward. "Get over here stat! Mr. Gray has gone berserk and is tearing up the ward." I jumped into my golf cart, put it in high gear and raced through the labyrinth of corridors to reach the General Surgery Head and Neck Ward. It took me five minutes from the time I received the call.

The wards in the VA hospital were open with ten beds on each side. There was considerable space down the middle of the ward. Mr. Gray was standing in the center of the ward picking up beds and tossing them as if flowers in a basket. This happened to anyone who got near him. The nurse and patients were in a panic for their own safety as well as this patient's life.

He had acute airway obstruction and was quickly becoming oxygen depleted. He would soon lose consciousness from an accumulation of carbon dioxide as a result of inability to exchange air. His color was changing from blue to black and the veins in his neck were bulging. We were watching a man go through the final stages of asphyxiation.

There was no way anyone could approach Mr. Gray in his present state. I waited patiently for the right moment and was prepared with a tracheotomy set opened and ready to move in. Within moments, he collapsed to the floor. Mr. Gray was unconscious and close to death. Without local anesthesia, I made a stab wound in the mid-line of his neck over the trachea. Once the trachea was entered, a blast of air was released along with a spray of dark blood from the surgical trach incision. A tube was inserted and secured. Mr. Gray began to breath, his pink color returned and he regained consciousness. The emergency was over. The ultra sound treatment caused edema of his vocal cords that resulted in a near fatal outcome. The children treated with ultra sound all had tracheotomies, thus a secured airway.

Medical advances require trial and error, not every untoward sequel can be anticipated. This new experience with human research helped shape my philosophy. One can be a pioneer mountain climber and risk one's own life but a doctor should not expect to benefit from someone else's life.

The life of Mr. Gray was saved because I was there but I am reminded he would not have been in that situation had it not been for me. *"A wise man learns from the mistakes of others; a fool doesn't learn from his own." Proverbs*

33)   Prison Doctor

Believe it or not, I was a prison doctor in the Virginia State Penitentiary (VSP). The most important lesson learned was to behave and never wind up in jail. It was a frightening place. In my last year of residency, I was invited to accompany my teacher Paul Middleton to assist him operating on a patient, a VSP inmate. Middleton was the ENT consultant, a Head and Neck Cancer Specialist for VSP and scheduled a prisoner, with a life sentence, for a total Laryngectomy and neck dissection.

I had no idea what to expect. On the day of surgery, we arrived and parked outside the prison walls. We were greeted by the outside guard. He spoke to us through a bullet proof glass enclosure. He asked for our ID. Before buzzing us in, he indoctrinated us about the dos and don'ts.

Most of the inmates in this prison had been sentenced to 20 years to life, convicted of anything from bank robbery to murder. "Don't look at them, don't talk to them and don't ask them why they are in here!"

We were then allowed to enter a narrow corridor. The gate locked behind us. We were being monitored on a large bay of video screens that filled inside the control room. The gate in front of us opened and we walked through a finely manicured grassy common area. There were two men dressed in stripped pajamas playing chess. One was smoking a pipe. The pleasant aroma of the fresh cut grass and the tobacco smoke was prominent. I noticed that on the right side of the grassy commons area was a prison with bars along the second floor of a three-story brick building. I was told that this area where we were walking was for the best-behaved inmates, considered trustees. I was impressed with the quiet solitude; one could hear the birds chirping.

At the end of the path, straight ahead of us, we saw another three-story brick building; the infirmary-hospital, and operating room. We climbed three flights of stairs to reach the OR. It didn't look any different than what we were used to at MCV, the University Hospital until we began to realize that we were in a different world. Middleton asked if 2 units of blood were set up as requested. The response we got from the circulating nurse was the first reminder that we were in prison. "No problem, we have walking donors of every blood type already cross-matched. This saves storage space and is much faster than waiting for the lab".

The surgery was completed without a hitch. I took off my wedding band to scrub up and pinned it to my scrub shirt. After surgery, I accidently threw the shirt in the laundry hamper. The shirt with my ring went to the prison laundry. I told the trustee and he reassured me it would be returned. The next day, I returned to the prison to check on the patient. Sure enough, the ring had been returned. "Amazing, the honesty among these prisoners" I thought. The patient was doing great and receiving fantastic care by his co-inmates. I checked the chart for the nurse's notes. They were complete and in order. I asked the trustee to explain why the patient received blood. It was not ordered and there was no indication that there was bleeding.

He explained that the lab blood man (phlebotomist) took blood every hour and took so much that he transfused the patient to replace the blood taken. The trustee noticed that this was disturbing to me and was a departure from normal medical protocols. He further explained, "The man who takes blood is also a lifer for beating his aunt to death with a broom handle because she pissed him off. He must be kept busy and he has the perfect job. Don't worry! We have an unlimited amount of blood. In this prison there is a large pool of walking donors who give blood in exchange for drugs. "

"That brings up one more practice here in prison. The patient requested that you double his narcotic orders. In the prison hospital, the patient gets half of what the doctor orders and the other half goes into the fund. Do you get me doc?" I went home that night happy to get my ring back but shocked by prison rules.

The next day, I was supposed to return to the prison to check on the patient. The morning newspaper reported that the prison doctor and three inmates were stabbed to death. This occurred in the three- story brick building set aside for the well-behaved inmates. The murders were part of a drug distribution conflict. I never showed up that day and vowed never to return.

Prison life was not for me.

Chapter 4

Military Doctor

34)   In the Army Now

July of 1966, I arrived in San Antonio Texas and reported to authorities at Ft. Sam Houston. After my family, wife and three little children were settled in their temporary quarters, I was shipped out to some remote camp on the outskirts of town for basic training.

We had four weeks of classroom and field work at Camp Bullis. We learned how to read a map, navigate at night by compass and stars, parade in step with 50 other doctor recruits, fire a rifle without killing the nearest guy, make a bed by tucking in the corners, polish shoes and shine brass belt buckles, who to salute and how to salute. Oh, I forgot to mention, eat everything served, and get used to complete lack of privacy. Some of us were to be shipped out to Vietnam either after completing basic training or after a year assigned "state side".

Classroom work wasn't too bad. Marching in cadence and in step was my biggest challenge. Remember, I had to deal with the dyslexia issue (Story #2). For me left and right were reversed, as was forward and backward. It became obvious to the drill Sergeant that the platoon would benefit most if I stayed in the stands for spectators.

I performed poorly on the firing range. The fact that I didn't shoot any friends was admirable. My problem was that I never hit the target. No one got upset and I was relieved to be washed out as a rifleman. After all, I was recruited to be a doctor.

Shining shoes and buckles seemed difficult for me. The brass-off solution and black shoe polish somehow splashed off beyond the intended boundaries. My khaki pants showed stains around the buckle and bottoms of my pants. I never passed inspection. If only someone would have clued me in to take off the belt and shoes before the polishing process. I never learned how to recognize rank, so I saluted every one.

Boot camp at Bullis tested my survival skills. You would think that my mom prepared me. Growing up, I was forced to eat everything; peas, carrots, broccolis, grilled liver, and even fried onions with shmaltzy chicken fat referred to as gribenes.

In the army, grub (food) was always served with a giant ladle. I mean everything was scooped out and dumped into my personal pot contained in my mess kit. Each morning we lined up on the mess line. Stacks of eggs were cracked open, placed into a large pot, mixed and spread over a large hot grill. The thick sticky mix was swiped back and forth a couple of times. This semi-liquid lumpy mixture was supposed to imitate scrambled eggs. The army chef's morning specialty was dumped onto my metal mess pot. I never liked eggs or anything from a chicken, so I walked over to a large garbage can that stood conspicuously at the end of the mess line. The can was labeled "slop can". I kid you not.

A large serving of "Shit on a Shingle", or SOS, was everyone's favorite and actually considered a treat. This delicacy is made with dried chipped beef, beef stock, and milk sauce served over a biscuit. Of all the food served in the army, this dish has a mouth watering aroma, rich flavor and a pleasing consistency, otherwise army food was not appealing to me.

My selective diet created little in and little out. Over the two weeks at Camp Bullis, I lost 15 pounds. In spite of my restricted diet, one still needs to take care of business. In the army everyone knew how to locate the latrine, just follow one's senses. However, it was rarely used by me. Even if I could or had the need, I couldn't overcome my modesty. There was no way to take care of business sitting on the can with ten other guys. You are correct; after two weeks at Camp Bullis, my face was noticeably greenish yellow in color and there were considerable abdominal discomfort from distension. Can the reader imagine my situation if I ate three squares a day? The army knew what they were doing; a fighting force has no time for daily needs.

Night evasion exercises were fun but dependent on a clever partner. Lee Rosky was such a partner. We were blindfolded and dropped off deep in the forest. To figure out where we were, we had to apply our classroom exercises to locate our position. We used our fluorescent lighted compass, read topography maps, and applied a protractor to the coordinates on the map together with the location of stars. We were simulating landing behind enemy lines and finding our way back to base without being captured. It turned out that our lack of navigation skills worked to our advantage. It seemed as soon as we turned on our low detection red light to read our map and compass, we were immediately captured, driven back to base in a jeep, given a mug of hot chocolate and allowed to hit the sack while the rest of our platoon played hide and seek for the rest of the freezing night.

Lee Rosky, my brilliant partner, got a heads up from some docs that took the course previously. The professional career soldiers who dropped us off knew exactly where we were from the outset. Can the reader imagine the headlines in the San Antonio Times, "Two Doctor Recruits Lost in the Forest During Night Exercises." Lee reasoned correctly, it is better if they find us without too much delay.

Actually, I was saved from revealing my serial number, we were never asked. In class we were drilled, if captured according to Geneva Convention, the rules of war require giving only name, rank and serial number. Even if they tortured me I would never reveal my serial number. Once again, my dyslexia prevented me from remembering more than four consecutive numbers.

Our week at Camp Bullis produced one tragic casualty. Each morning at 6am the loudspeaker would loudly blare out a rendition of the song Lili Marlene. This awakened all of the exhausted doctor recruits except one, the recently graduated anesthesiologist. He was single and scheduled to leave for Vietnam upon completion of basic training. He seemed to deteriorate as each day passed. He became less responsive and more withdrawn. We noticed that he was easily startled and his speech became altered; he now stammered and stuttered.

One morning, we found him under his cot curled up in a fetal position. He was taken away and never seen again. We were told he received a medical discharge, unfit to serve.

On a happy note, our daily morning song can still be heard in my memory. I actually enjoyed it. Curiously, it was sung by a popular German entertainer, Marlene Dietrich. The song was popular among Germans as well as allied troops during WWII. It has a haunting melody and tells of the yearning soldier requesting that his loved one at home wait a little longer for his return. I commend the reader to listen to the song Lili Marlene on YouTube.

Except for the one chap, we all survived boot camp and I, for one, was looking forward to rejoin my family and most of all, for some privacy.

During my service in the military, the Vietnam War raged on. Those of us who stayed "state side" were constantly reminded of the horrible conditions over there and were grateful to have our shipping out orders delayed.

After the military, Lee Rosky practiced Gastroenterology in Egg Harbor Township, Atlantic City Hospital and Shore Memorial Hospital in Somers Point. Lee became a gifted teacher and a sought after speaker.

35)   Letters from Vietnam, 1966

I met Ron Spielman while training to be a soldier at Camp Bullis. He had just finished his Ophthalmology residency and was recruited as part of the Berry Plan. Both Ron and Lee were friends growing up in Atlantic City, NJ, fraternity brothers at Franklin and Marshall College, and were residents together at Thomas Jefferson University Hospital in Philadelphia. We had a mutual friend, Stan Schiff. They included me in their clan and we became close; the military is a great place for bonding. Ron was chosen to ship out to Vietnam (VN) right after graduating from Bullis.

We kept in touch by mail. His experience related in his letters made me realize the stark contrast between his assignment and mine. This is his story.

Ron worked with the 85th Evacuation Hospital Medical Team stationed in Que Nhon located close to the DMZ (demilitarized zone) near the border between North and South VN. It was a patch of jungle near the South China Sea until the 2nd Cav carved out a two- mile fortress. There was a 10 mile perimeter lit up at night by search lights placed every 30 meters and protected by machine gun nests and strategically placed land mines. Three combat helicopters with 50 caliber machine guns and rocket launching capabilities patrolled the base on a constant basis.

This was the largest helicopter base in VN. 450 of these helicopters designed for combat were maintained at this facility. In addition to the fighting machines, there was a fleet of helicopter troop transports. The men on the base referred to the place as the golf course because the perimeter was pocked with holes from mortar attacks. Needless to say, no one kept a score card in this place. Mortar attacks were a nightly occurrence.

When a Mortar Attack was announced, there was a drill. Everyone was required to run for their helmet, flack vest, and weapon. Ron's job was to head to the receiving ward. The receiving ward was part of the hospital complex; 6 Quonset huts protected by piled up sand bags. There were 4 operating rooms, three postoperative wards and one receiving ward. According to Ron, they were all well equipped.

This base had 8 general surgeons, 4 medical officers, one ortho guy, many corpsmen, nurses, and Red Cross volunteers. Ron was the only Ophthalmologist and he questioned the military's judgment. He was convinced that he would have been more useful at a tertiary facility where he could evaluate and treat eye conditions, the disorders for which he spent four years preparing. Instead, he was relegated to administer first aid and serve as a triage officer or first surgical assistant.

He wrote that life was great if one enjoys camping and adventure. Stationed at a huge helicopter base, he could hop a ride anywhere in Vietnam. However, he was hesitant to take advantage of this perk for fear that he could be shot down in the process. He related that there was a lot of down time, time to regret his isolation in a surreal world and time for boredom and waves of depression.

Ron slept on a cot covered with a net to keep out mosquitoes and rats. His tent had a dirt floor and was to be his quarters for the next 12 months. The May to November monsoon rains presented a problem for a tent dweller. There was flooding; an actual stream and rapids flowed under his cot. The rains brought puddles and pools for mosquitoes to breed. The mosquitoes carried malaria and this was countered by daily doses of quinine, the nastiest tasting stuff that you can imagine. Ron rationalized that the bad taste was better than contracting malaria. There were also large hungry rats that come out of the jungle to eat the garbage. Ron counted on the night net to keep the rats away.

He was kept busy running daily sick calls, occasionally called to suture a laceration or manage a Pungi stick puncture. The VC (Viet Cong) harassed our troops who were sent out on patrol. Along the jungle trails they placed camouflaged sharpened bamboo poles smeared with human feces. These injuries were common and could be deadly if untreated.

Two months after arriving for duty, Ron had his first night of indoctrination and a night that will always haunt him the rest of his days.

It was November, late in the afternoon. The clouds were low lying and the humidity was thick as soup when the torrential tropical monsoon rains turned the ground into bogs of mud and grime. Under better weather conditions, three helicopter crews circled above the base. They called in warnings of mortar attacks stating the enemy's position by exact coordinates that allowed an almost instantaneous response from 8 inch and 175 mm guns. On this night the patrolling copters were grounded, poor visibility. "Mortar attack!" announced the loud speakers all over the base.

There was a direct hit on the mechanics' tent. Twenty young Americans were smoking, playing cards, and drinking booze when the explosion hit them. Ron followed the rules for the mortar drill. At the receiving-triage hut it was bedlam. Three were (DOA) dead on arrival from fatal head wounds. There was a group of young men with limbs ripped off. The rest were shredded with metal fragments that penetrated their chest and abdominal structures. The general surgeons saved the lives of most of the wounded.

Ron related that this was his busiest night performing surgery. Three shredded eyes could not be saved and required removal.

On this gruesome evening, the mass butchering of healthy young men, transformed Ron into an emotional state of shock. Once things settled down and there was time to reflect, Ron began to convulse with emotional pain. He realized that two of the eyes he removed belonged to one soldier. Ron was unable sleep peacefully the rest of his tour in VN.

After reading Ron's account of a real war zone, I realized that whatever I saw as a "state side" doctor can never match the horrors of war on the battle field.

Ron Spielman practiced Ophthalmology in South Florida until 2014. I spoke to him on the telephone not long ago. He was so happy to speak with me and affectionately remembers me as "Big Nose". It is fascinating what we remember. It has been 52 years since he sent me letters from Vietnam.

36)   Doctors Make the Worst Patients

William Amaral was a career army officer, a lieutenant colonel, board certified in Oro-Maxillo- Facial surgery and Chief of the Dental Service at Darnell Army Hospital. We first met in the hospital emergency room where he was called in to evaluate a soldier with a fractured jaw. I was there to control a nose bleed. Normally, we both would have preferred to see these patients in our respective clinics but it was after hours. It was more convenient to manage these patients in the ER where there were support personnel. The nose bleed was minor. A cotton pledget with Vaseline placed in the left nasal passage held in place with tape solved the problem.

Amaral was waiting for the radiographs of his patient's jaw. I caught his attention and introduced myself. He was personable and friendly. I told him of my background working with Elmer Bear (Story #18). He perked up recognizing Bear as a leader in the field of maxillo-facial trauma. Colonel Amaral invited me to visit his clinic.

This friendship blossomed into a close working arrangement and mutual respect. I offered to work with him in his clinic one half day a week; he accepted.

He taught me the "army way" and slowly convinced me that office surgery was preferred. I was amazed how his conservative approach avoided the need for general anesthesia, time in the OR and hospitalization; these options were rarely required. These measures were essential in the military where the goal was to get the soldier back to duty with minimal delay. Besides, in the military there were limited resources, equipment and personnel as will be demonstrated in stories #36-40.

Neither Atiyeh nor Bear had military exposure and the "army way" was definitely not their way. Before Amaral, I was taught that adequate reduction of facial fractures required incisions over the fracture sites, drilling holes, threading and tightening the wires to hold the bones together. The Bear- Atiyeh approach was universally accepted in civilian practice. These non-military approaches required OR time and hospitalization; a completely different philosophy.

Wednesdays, from 2pm to 4pm was facial fracture clinic with Amaral. The first thing I learned was to distinguish function from form. Function meant accurate occlusion so a patient could chew. Almost all jaw fractures encountered in the military could be repaired as an outpatient and the soldier returned to duty on the day of surgery. Form was how it looked pre-op compared to post-op. In the army, it was primarily function. Soldiers were rarely concerned how it looks. For example, an uncorrected broken nose added character; made a guy look tough and sexy.

Fractures of the zygomatic arch that caused an indentation in front of the ear or impacted on the chewing muscle and limited opening the jaw was corrected. The inside of the cheek was anesthetized with local and a heavy metal instrument was pushed through the mucosa and under the depressed bone. Then, the bone was lifted and the depression eliminated by checking with discerning fingers placed over the depression. If the depression was corrected and the jaw movement limitation was relieved, the patient was discharged back to duty.
In the army, pre and post- operative photographs and radiographs were not taken. "How is this possible?", I asked. Amaral explained, "These are young healthy macho men, trained for combat, no complainers, and the most important factor is, no lawyers.

While working with Amaral, my impacted third molars acted up. He detected the presence of pericoronitis bilaterally. This occurs when a flap of gingival (gum) tissue grows over the partially erupted tooth and forms a pocket. Food collects in the pocket, decays and emits an unpleasant order, referred to as Halitosis.

Amaral explained that this condition was common. His diagnosis and explanation impressed me. "When do you want to do it?" I asked. He replied, "The "army way" is not to hesitate. Now is a good time."

I recalled my terrible experience when I was 8 years old. My mom, trying to save money, took me to a high school chum who became a dentist. Granted, it was a decayed baby tooth that should have come out with a yank, a twist, and a tug. However, in my case, it wasn't so easy. At least that's how I remembered it. It turns out that this friend of my mom never practiced dentistry as preferred by his mother. He took up plumbing instead. I should have suspected by his dirty finger nails that he wasn't a real dentist. Further, I never saw a dentist use that kind of pliers, they were definitely plumber's pliers. I will never forget his death grip; his muscular arm vice that held my head in place while he ripped my tooth out. I swore never again.

I had so much confidence in Amaral that I consented to four third molar extractions right then. Amaral called my wife, shared the plans and agreed to take me home when the surgery was completed.

He gave me a heavy dose of sedative. Once that kicked in, I don't remember receiving the local injections. I do remember Amaral warning me that I would feel pressure, which I did, but there was never any pain. I woke up in my bed. My mouth was bloody, my cheeks were swollen and the dull aching was unrelenting. I continued with pain medicine for three weeks and didn't return to work for a month.

Doctors make the worst patients.

Working with Amaral converted me to the "army way". Unfortunately, my euphoria for army medicine was short lived and lasted until I returned to civilian life. Nevertheless, many of the principles learned from Amaral were incorporated into the way I managed patients after being in the army.

37)   Frontal Abscess

I entered the military as a captain in the United States Army Medical Corp. The next two years were among the best times for me as a doctor. All military personnel had free access to medical care and there were no concerns about lawsuits.

After six weeks of basic training, the Army assigned me to Fort Hood, Darnell Army Hospital. The Fort was located on the outskirts of a small remote army town, Killeen Texas. The nearest towns were Lampasas and Waco, Texas.

Fort Hood was the home of the United States Armored Corps. The base was the size of the State of Rhode Island. It was large enough to simulate tank battles and fire an Honest John Surface to Surface Rocket as far as 16 miles without leaving the base. On base there were two armored divisions with over 350,000 personnel. This included combatants, support staff, and retired military.

My excitement and anticipation was palpable. The time had come for me to apply what I had learned. Like most new things, expectations are often not realized. A military outpost like Darnell Hospital served as a first aid station. Serious problems were transported to the Army Medical Center in Ft. Sam Houston located in San Antonio, Texas, 146 miles down U.S. Route 35, a two- and- a half hour ride by ambulance or twenty minutes by helicopter.

The ENT Clinic was scheduled from 10 to 12 in the morning and 2 to 4 in the afternoon. When I arrived to the clinic on my first day, there were only nine soldiers sitting on a long bench outside the clinic waiting to be seen.

Tingle, a career corpsman, efficiently diagnosed and treated each young man and finished the clinic in less than an hour. The system was designed to screen the fakers who tried to avoid the discomforts of harsh military life. It was not fun to be out in the field eating canned rations and sleeping in a trench with insects and rattle snakes. Tingle was an expert in this screening process. This career corpsman knew his stuff after over twenty years in the military.

I waited to be consulted by Tingle who managed the clinic alone in his usual manner. After the last soldier was returned to duty, Tingle would report, "Captain May, sir, morning clinic – no problems. I'll clean up and see you back for afternoon session at 2."

Naturally, I was disappointed to be replaced with a corpsman. This was easily understood after I looked at the patient log for the morning clinic. The diagnoses included URI and stuffy nose, traumatic nose bleed, external otitis, viral laryngitis and post-firing range tinnitus referred for hearing tests.

After reviewing the outpatient clinic log, I glanced at the surgical schedule. The ENT service was permitted to schedule surgery one half day per week and only if OR time was available. Our surgery schedule for the next six months consisted of T & A (tonsil & adenoidectomies).

When I discovered that the doctor that preceded me was an OJT (On- the- Job- Trainee) it all made sense. An OJT after graduating medical school spent six weeks with an ENT specialist at Ft. Sam Houston or Walter Reed Hospital in Washington DC and was then sent to an outpost like Darnell. I was his replacement.

I asked Tingle, "Out of 350,000 personnel on this base, how is it possible only nine men showed up for clinic?" His answer was unacceptable for me, "Captain, sir, that's the system."

The next day, I insisted that I sit in with Tingle. It didn't take long to realize that a corpsman or an OJT did not replace a board-certified ENT specialist.

A young soldier with the URI and stuffy nose, who was evaluated the day before, returned because his frontal headache had gotten worse. It was apparent to my trained eye that the diagnosis was acute frontal sinusitis with subperiosteal abscess, a potentially life threatening condition. This meant the sinus deep to the forehead bone located at the level of the eyebrows harbored a smoldering abscess. The infection eroded through the bone and now there was a collection of pus under the skin of the forehead. In the same way, the infection would have been able reach the brain through the back wall of the frontal sinus; which was potentially a life- threatening condition.

I instructed Tingle to accompany this man to Radiology and obtain a sinus series. I instructed him to be sure to include a film of the frontal sinus with the patient's forehead against the X-ray machine. This technique yields the most accurate reproduction of the actual size of the frontal sinus. I stressed that I will need this image for the surgery. Once this task was completed, Tingle brought him back to the clinic.

A review of the radiographs showed the frontal sinus was opaque and confirmed my diagnosis. Tingle was impressed.

The soldier was admitted to the hospital and IV antibiotics were started. A spinal tap showed that the fluid was clear and the pressure normal. These findings indicated that the infection had not extended through the thin posterior wall of the frontal sinus into the intra cranial space. In 1966, CT Scans and MRI imaging had not yet been invented.

After twelve hours of antibiotics, the pain persisted and the redness and swelling over the forehead was doughy and extremely tender. This man needed surgical drainage. The threat of intracranial spread, meningitis, brain abscess and death could follow if the condition remained untreated.

I called the OR scheduling clerk. He handed the phone to the "mean" Sergeant Nurse who controlled the OR. She made it clear to me that ENT had no OR time even though I pleaded that this was a surgical emergency. Without detailing the back and forth with her, she made it clear that the answer was no. Her final response, "If this is a surgical emergency then transfer the patient to San Antonio." Tingle knew the system. "Call Cornel Ashby, he is the CEO."

I called, introduced myself and explained the situation. "Can you do it?" he asked. "Yes, sir!" I replied. "Call the OR and inform

them to clear a room for you. If you need anything call me
back."

The OR staff of corpsmen and nurses were astounded that what
they thought would be a simple incision and drainage was a
craniotomy without exposing the brain. I requested a
craniotomy set used for a neurosurgical procedure. There was
some initial resistance because no one at Darnel had ever
observed a fully certified Otolaryngologist in action. I had their
full cooperation because of Col. Ashby's orders.

I made a coronal incision over the top of the head from ear to
ear across the scalp. Pus under pressure was released and
poured over the operative site.

Bleeding was controlled with Ramey Neurosurgical metal clips
and an electrocautery. The scalp was elevated off the
periosteum (thin connective tissue barrier over the skull bone)
and draped over the eyes. The superior orbital rims (bony
prominences above the eye sockets) were palpated. There was
a defect in the bone over the front of the frontal sinus where
the infection had eroded through the bone and formed the sub
dermal abscess.

The size and configuration of the frontal sinus was determined
by placing the sterilized X-ray film taken before the surgery,
over the front of the skull.

An orthopedic bone saw, much like one that was used to take off a plaster cast, was used to outline the borders of the frontal sinus. A mallet and chisel completed the cut and the frontal bone of the frontal sinus was turned down, hinged on the periosteum above the orbits.

The pus that filed the sinus cavity was irrigated with an antibiotic solution. A rubber drain was placed from the frontal sinus into the nose and sutured to the nostril. All structures were sutured back in place. The procedure took two hours.

The "mean" nurse was humiliated and retreated into her office. This marked her declaration of war on ENT. However, I won the respect of the OR staff and Col. Ashby was delighted. There was no paper work required and no need for the expense of a helicopter. Col. Ashby welcomed me to his staff as a competent ENT surgeon.

I appreciated the support and confidence of Col. Ashby but most importantly, he never asked me if I ever performed a frontal osteoplastic procedure as in this case. I would have had to inform Col. Ashby that I assisted one time but never performed the procedure. There was a saying among the residents in training, "See one, do one and teach one."

There always had to be a first time.

38)   Whispering Soldier

Day to day things didn't change much at Ft. Hood, and when they did, folks took note. It snowed one day, just a dusting. This was such a rare phenomenon that drivers decompensated. That day, cars were slipping and sliding as personnel made their way to work. As expected, there were cars that were rear ended and then struck the car in front setting up a chain reaction.

The hospital ER was crowded with drivers and passengers that had scrapes and bruises. Fortunately, no one was seriously injured.

The ER was down the hall from the ENT clinic. I was about to enter the clinic to start a day's work and just then, a soldier who had been evaluated and discharged from the ER, passed by me.

His breathing was audibly strident and with each breath there was a distinct wheezing sound. He was thin, well over six feet tall, and had a long thin neck. I detected the crushed larynx sign, instead of a prominent Adam's apple or voice box, his neck was flat.

I stopped him, "How are you doing soldier?" He whispered. "Ok, I guess. The ER doc said I could return to duty and my voice would slowly improve."

I walked him to the OR and into an empty room and sat him up on the OR table. I ordered a nurse to bring me a tracheotomy set and local for injection. The soldier was reassured by my calm tone, "You must allow me to make an airway in your neck or you will die."

The "mean" OR nurse who was out to destroy me, seized the opportunity. She complained to Col. Ashby. The OR room that I chose was one being prepared for the Colonel. He was not happy about my outrageous behavior. He couldn't forgive bringing a fully clothed patient into a sterile environment and a surgeon performing surgery without scrubbing and without gloves. This was a total breakdown in standard procedure.

This was an absolute emergency. With each passing minute following this type of injury, the swelling within the voice box increases until the breathing passage is completely shut off.

The tracheotomy was performed with the patient sitting up because he would not have been able to breathe in the lying down position. The emergency was over after a twenty second stab wound tracheotomy.

No one said another word after witnessing this life saving procedure. Even the "mean" nurse was beginning to change her feelings towards me.

Col. Ashby cancelled his surgery and informed the OR staff to prepare the patient and operating room to complete the treatment for this young man as I had suggested.

Col. Ashby personally assisted me as I reconstructed the whispering soldier's crushed larynx. When the incisions were made and the area of the voice box was uncovered, the extent of the injury became apparent to all present. The voice box was severely crushed.

The OR staff was impressed with the manner in which I was able to wire the pieces of cartilage back together and reattach the vocal cords. The postoperative course was amazing. He was discharged without a trach tube and with a functional voice and airway. Col. Ashby realized that my unconventional behavior saved this soldier's life.

The management and outcome in this case was routine for me after six months in the "war zone" as an intern at Hahnemann and three years managing head and neck trauma on the ENT service at MCV.

This case of the whispering soldier was an example of a dead man walking. Some patients are not supposed to die.

39)   Face Off

Staff Sergeant "M" was returning from Killeen to Ft. Hood on a Friday night after downing more beers than he could remember.

According to the Texas State Trooper's report, the Sergeant attempted to cross the Lampasas River over a one lane iron trestle bridge. Instead of going between the girders, he drove into the side support structure. He was thrown through the windshield and avulsed the right side of his face. A minimum number of sutures were placed to close the wound.

General anesthesia and surgical repair was delayed several days because of his elevated blood alcohol level and poor general condition.

Three days later during surgery, one could appreciate the extent of the injury. The facial nerve was found divided. The ends were re-approximated, matching the proximal branches to the distal branches.

Six months later his wounds healed with minimal scaring and he recovered facial tone, symmetry, excellent eye closure, and a slightly asymmetrical smile.

The surgical staff at Darnell Army Hospital referred to this case as Face Off.

The new Otolaryngologist had established himself as the can-do guy to manage head and neck surgical challenges.

The success in this last case set the stage for the Tank Hatch Injury.

40)   Tank Hatch Injury

It was around 6:00 pm on a Wednesday night. There was dense fog and visibility was limited. General Abrams ordered his tank captain to lead six tanks out for night maneuvers. This tank captain was Abrams' top man from the Korean War. He served as Abrams' forward eyes and was the key to battle maneuver decisions.

As the captain, he had his head sticking out of the hatch to survey the battle field. The fog limited his view. As his M60 tank moved forward, it suddenly lurched to a halt. The tank had encountered an obstacle of some kind. The safety latch malfunctioned and the heavily armored hatch, a virtual manhole cover weighing around 120 pounds, came crashing down on the top of the captain's helmet. His chin was smashed into the hatch rim. He was found unconscious, extricated and transported to the Darnell Hospital. I received an urgent call and headed for the ER.

When I arrived, General Abrams was standing by his captain who was sitting up on a gurney. The captain had regained consciousness and was talking coherently. This was a favorable sign.

He had a total left facial paralysis and clear liquid dripping out of his left ear canal. The ear drum was torn. Eye movements were normal and the rest of the cranial nerves had been spared. I explained to General Abrams and Col. Ashby, the Hospital Commandant who had just arrived, my findings and recommendations.

The Captain has a fractured jaw involving the part closest to his left ear. The ear bone was also fractured. The roof of the ear bone forms the plate of bone between the ear and brain cavity. This was fractured allowing brain fluid to flow out through the ear canal. This defect in the bone needed to be repaired. The facial nerve and the hearing bones were disrupted and also needed to be repaired.

The reader must keep in mind, these findings were based on physical findings and plain X-ray films of the skull and mandible.

Imaging studies like CT scans or MRI had not yet been invented in 1966.

My recommendation was surgical repair without delay. This tank commander was precious and like a family member to General Abrams. He wanted the best treatment available.

Col. Ashby wanted this patient evacuated by helicopter to San Antonio to get the best care by the experts at Fort Sam Houston. A call was made to make the arrangements. Col. Ashby was informed that helicopter transport was not an option because of the dense fog and limited visibility. Further, he was told that ground transportation with the weather conditions would also be hazardous.

Ashby asked me, "Can you do it?" "Yes, sir", I replied. "What do you need?" He asked.

I explained that ear surgery was not performed at Darnell because we didn't have the proper instruments. I told Ashby, "The necessary ear equipment could be borrowed from the Scott and White Ear Clinic in Waco Texas, 60 miles up the road." I made a list: a complete set of ear instruments, a high speed drill with new cutting and diamond burs, and a binocular operating microscope with a teaching side arm.

This was a dream come true. I had been bugging the "mean" OR nurse to acquire ear instruments and an operating microscope since arriving on base six months ago. Her response had been "If you ask one more time, you will be sent to Vietnam."

General Abrams notified Scott and White Clinic that a two and a half ton, 6x6 cargo truck had been dispatched to pick up the list of items requested. The administrator at Scott and White was told it was a military emergency and he complied.

The surgery began at 1 am and took five hours. Ashby and Abrams took turns looking through the teaching side arm attached to the microscope. I explained each step and pointed out the structures. They were fascinated by the intricacies and details of this anatomy.

The middle ear contains the ossicles (Malleus, Incus & Stapes) and facial nerve. The brain and brain fluid sit above the roof of the middle ear. In the case of the "Tank Hatch Injury" the jaw was pushed back and up into the middle ear.

Each fracture was uncovered. Fascia (a thin transparent sheet of connective tissue) from over the temporalis muscle (chewing muscle located on the side of the head) was taken from above the ear. This tissue was used to repair the brain fluid leak. The facial nerve was compressed and partially disrupted by a bone fragment. The bone fragments were removed; the ends of the facial nerve were freshened and re-approximated. The Incus, one of the three tiny ear bones, was displaced and repositioned. The torn ear drum was repaired.

Colonel Amaral, a career officer who was the chief of maxilla-facial surgery, was consulted for the jaw fracture. In his experience an un-displaced fracture of this type would correct itself and no direct intervention was necessary.

General Abram's Captain recovered and was discharged on the fifth PO day. After six weeks, the ear drum was healed and his hearing was restored to almost normal. He returned to active duty.

General Abrams expressed his appreciation. My wife and I were among his honored guests at his annual Christmas Party. We were greeted at the door by his wife. "A special table was prepared for you. Everything on this table was brought from San Antonio and is strictly kosher"

I followed the captain's post-operative course for six months. Facial function began to recover after three months. After six months, he demonstrated excellent symmetrical tone, eye lid closure, and a smile that was weaker on the injured side. Six months after the surgery, General Abrams and his tank captain shipped out to Vietnam.

I spent my second year at Darnell and was never sent to Vietnam, which was unusual. I will always wonder if this decision was related to the case of the "Tank Hatch Injury".

Chapter 5

Academics

41)   <u>Picture Taker</u>

In July of 1968 I completed my military obligation and began an NIH (National Institute of Health) Head and Neck Cancer Surgery Fellowship at Washington University in St. Louis, MO.

A year studying in Professor Joseph Ogura's World Famous Department would be a career changing opportunity for me. Doctor Ogura's approach to surgical management of throat cancer was unique. He developed procedures that successfully removed the cancer and preserved voice and swallowing function.

I joined a highly competitive stable of over achievers. The residents spent a year in the department of General Surgery, a year in the animal laboratory doing research and four years with Dr. Ogura on the ENT Surgical Service. This program produced super doctors and future department chairmen.

The staff and residents taught me the system. All patients admitted to the ENT service at Barnes Hospital (the ENT designated Hospital at Washington University) belonged to Dr. Ogura. These patients were operated upon exclusively by Dr.

Ogura's residents. Staff and Fellows were not permitted to touch a surgical knife. For me, this meant that I would not have an opportunity to gain surgical experience. This rule was enforced by Dr. Ogura's first deputy, Hugh Biller and was adhered to by all. Attending and supervising surgery was reserved for senior staff members.

This set up presented me with a huge challenge. If I was not able to operate then I had to figure out a way to watch Ogura's head and neck procedures. Taking pictures became my OR admission ticket. Ogura needed pictures of his surgical innovations to be used for lectures and publications.

Doctor Ogura could devise and perform the most intricate and sophisticated surgical procedures but couldn't grasp the essentials of photography... focus, exposure and composition.

Ogura wasn't the only surgeon with this handicap. Clinical cameras for dummies became popular for surgeons. There were all kinds of attachments that fit on the end of a camera. The insertion of a particular metal frame focused the camera. The frames were color coded. For example, a red frame was used for close, blue for medium and yellow for a far shot. The close shot was for a small field while the far shot encompassed the entire surgical field. This feature provided a well- focused picture but the exposure and composition were not consistent.

Other easy set ups included cameras with color-coded lenses that fit on the camera. Another was the introduction of ring lights that attached to the front of the camera. These cameras for dummies were adequate for surface shots but not for pictures of subjects in a cavity like the tympanic membrane (ear drum), vocal cords and pulmonary bronchi (tubes that bring air into the lungs).

In 1941, Holinger, an ENT Endoscopist from Chicago made a major contribution when he introduced the Holinger-Brubaker endoscopic camera. However, the camera had limitations; it was big and bulky. Further, the camera required a pulley system installed in the OR to suspend this monster camera. Imagine managing a box the size of a medium microwave appliance that weighed thirty-five pounds.

This endoscopic camera contraption was constructed by Brubaker, who was a machinist and a patient of Holinger's. Brubaker designed the camera according to Holinger's specifications.

A silver tube attached to the camera lens extended out of the device. This was designed to capture an image at the end of the tube. The tubes were two different sizes. There was a tube to view the vocal cords and a longer tube that could be inserted passed the vocal cords into the trachea, which then advanced to the pulmonary bronchi.

Brubaker made only three of these cameras, one for Holinger, one for Jackson, an ENT Endoscopist in Philadelphia, and one for Max Som, a Head and Neck Cancer Surgeon in NYC. As one could have predicted, this specialized camera that was capable of capturing one of a kind photographs never became popular. The monster camera was not only unwieldy, but a bit pricey at 3500 dollars.

Max Som was a close associate of Dr. Ogura. They were both world recognized head and neck cancer specialists. When Ogura saw Som's clear and vivid pictures of laryngeal cancer, he was impressed. Ogura borrowed the camera but could never get it to work.

I discovered the camera in Ogura's office one day. It was just sitting in the bottom of a closet filled with boxes of unlabeled slides and a variety of "dummy" cameras.

Ogura would not admit that he was unsuccessful in mastering any of these gadgets. I inquired about the monster Brubaker camera. "Leave it alone. The damn thing doesn't work. That's why Som tried to pan it off on me. I never paid for it and Som never asked me for the $3500 he paid Brubaker."

I insisted that the camera, if I could figure how to work it, would be useful in the animal lab for documenting my research. Ogura liked this idea.

The illumination was provided by a large flash bulb used by press photographers. After each picture, the bulb had to be replaced. These bulbs were expensive. The camera used a roll of Kodak film, rated at the slowest speed, ASA 25, and allowed for only 20 exposures. Today, it's so much simpler with digital photography giving the photographer almost unlimited options in exposure settings and number of pictures recorded on a memory card.

The Brubaker-Holinger big silver box housed a German made, high end Leica camera. I discovered why Ogura never got it to work. The camera came with instructions written in German. It was impossible to open and load the film without the directions.

Ruedi Thalmann, a German born PhD who worked in the department, translated the instructions and directed me through the steps to properly install the film.

The camera took perfect pictures. Before showing the results of my efforts to Dr. Ogura, there was a modification that could save the cost of replacing expensive press photographer's flash bulbs.

I had the device's conventional light source converted to an electronic flash. A capacitor was installed.

After it was plugged into an electrical outlet, 4000 volts would build up in seconds and discharge upon pressing a button located in the black pistol handle. With a "poof" a bright burst of light was directed down the silver Brubaker tube that illuminated the subject. The picture produced was spectacular in terms of the color, shadows, depth and contrast.

Now, I was ready to make my presentation to Ogura. I had a series of slides of pictures taken in the lab of a dog's vocal cords. He was truly impressed.

"May, tomorrow bring the camera to the OR, I have three patients with throat cancer scheduled for a laryngeal examination and biopsy."

Naturally, since I was the one to get the camera to work, I assumed that I would be the best one to take the pictures. Finally! My ticket into the OR had arrived, I thought.

The camera was heavy and bulky and we didn't have a pulley system installed. The big silver box containing the camera and newly installed capacitor was placed on a mobile metal OR instrument table. The table was stainless steel, had four sturdy legs and rolled on rubber wheels. As soon as the camera was plugged into the OR wall socket, a hum became audible as the capacitor charged to 4000 volts.

I asked Ogura to allow me to take the picture but he insisted that he do it himself. I suggested that he place the silver tube into position and when he was satisfied, I would take over. He insisted that he do the photography without any assistance and pushed me aside.

Ogura was struggling to line up the silver tube extending out of the monster camera and the patient's mouth. The position of the tube was fixed by the height of the instrument table. The ideal position required raising or lowering the operating table. After some considerable effort, Dr. Ogura lined up everything to view the throat cancer. General anesthesia helped relax the patient and relieved any discomfort.

By now, the OR was crowded with observers; first time events always attracted curiosity seekers. Ogura pressed the button and 4000 volts of electrical charge was released.

Boom! Sparks! The room filled with smoke and the odor of burnt rubber. In the meantime, Dr. Ogura was frozen to the metal on the side of the camera box. I immediately pulled the plug out of the wall. With this action, the electrical circuit was interrupted. The camera was pulled out of the patient's mouth and came to rest on top of the mobile table. Fortunately, Dr. Ogura's hands were not injured; they were protected from electrical burns by his latex OR gloves.

The scene was frightening. The OR emptied as the panicked staff in total disarray tried to escape the chaos of the smoke-filled room.

Reality set in when I heard Dr. Ogura scream, "Get that camera out of here and May, you are banned from the OR!" "There goes my career as an Ogura trained Head and Neck Cancer surgeon" I thought.

Although it didn't end well for me, there was much for which to be grateful. From that moment on, electrical safety required that all appliances used in the OR be grounded. The monster camera was never cleared for use in the OR; it did not even have a three- pronged plug.

The fact that the camera was mounted on a metal table with rubber wheels saved Ogura from possible death by electrocution. Imagine what could have happened if the 4000 volts went through Ogura instead of escaping down the legs of the table and melting the four rubber wheels into the OR floor! This was the source of the burnt rubber odor.

After two- weeks, I was pardoned and once again permitted to enter the OR. Ogura realized that my camera caper was well intentioned and I was the only one who came to his rescue. However, the monster camera received a life time sentence to spend its remaining days on the bottom of the closet.

42)   <u>Admission Ticket to the OR</u>

Ogura hired a full- time professional photographer, Dave Bellucci, who was on call 24/7 to document planned surgery as well as the unexpected. I made a deal with Dave to be his assistant, whenever he was scheduled or called to the OR, he contacted me.

Dave used a single lens reflex Nikon camera. As his assistant, I purchased a Nikon camera just like the pro. This relationship taught me medical photography and provided me with an admission ticket to the OR. Ogura never noticed me looking over Dave's shoulder whenever a picture was requested. This way, I was able to have a clear view of the essential steps of the surgery and snapped my own pictures.

Dave notified me that there was a big case scheduled for the next day. Ogura was planning a first time ever procedure for a patient with an unusual challenge. We were told to be prepared to take lots of pictures. Ogura stressed that he planned to present this case at the next International head and neck symposium scheduled in two weeks.

On the OR view box, Dr. Ogura posted a drawing of the patient's condition. In this case, the cancer extended across the anterior commissure to the left vocal cord where the vocal cords formed a "V".

A total laryngectomy (complete removal of the voice box) and the creation of a hole in the neck was the conventional treatment for this condition. The location called for a total laryngectomy because of anatomical considerations as well as the tumor's biological behavior. Cancer in this location often spreads along a fibrous band or ligament to the neck outside the voice box.

Ogura had devised a procedure to remove this extensive cancer and restore the voice without jeopardizing breathing or swallowing. A crowd of staff and visiting doctors showed up in order to watch the master perform this new procedure. Ogura spotted Dave, his private professional clinical photographer, and told the onlookers to move aside. We had a position reserved next to Ogura.

Ogura drew the lines on the patient's neck for the incision using a gentian violate sterile felt pen. He stepped aside and Dave took the picture. A flash was not necessary, the OR lights were quite adequate.

The initial incision was made, the bleeding was controlled and the blood from the incision was wiped clean. Ogura, again, stepped aside and indicated to Dave to take another picture. Each time Dave snapped his picture, I took a picture over Dave's shoulder.

This went on with each step of the surgery. The time required to perform the procedure was lengthened considerably. Normally, Ogura did not take the time to clean up the surgical field between each step. Dave learned to take pictures that had bloody sponges, bloody instruments and surgeons' bloody gloved hands in the field. I had to constantly remind Ogura that these pictures were to be shown to an international audience and had to be perfect. Ogura was reminded with each photo opportunity to clean up the field. Although it was not the way he preferred to operate, he complied with a grumble.

The procedure was near completion and Bellucci looked pale. His surgical cap was soaked in perspiration. This was uncharacteristic for Dave. He never perspired during an OR shoot. The room was cool and Dave hadn't physically exerted himself taking the pictures. Something was wrong!

Then, as Dave advanced the film in his camera to 40 exposures, the problem became clear to me. Normally, his camera was loaded with a 36 picture roll of film. Either, the film in Dave's camera wasn't loaded correctly or, in his excitement, he failed to load his camera with film!

Dave looked at Ogura and Ogura looked at Dave. I reassured Ogura that Dave had to reload. In the meantime, I would complete the photographic documentation. Ogura never learned Bellucci's secret of the empty camera; the pictures that

I took over Dave's shoulder satisfied Ogura's expectations. He was pleased with the photos.

Dave and I continued to work together with greater respect than ever and Ogura appreciated how I filled in. I became Ogura's official backup Nikon Camera Picture Taker.

At the completion of my fellowship, I had a complete book with drawings, notes and pictures of each procedure performed by Dr. Ogura. This book would be my bible for the rest of my surgical career.

43)   Banished to the Animal Lab

In 1969, after completion of my year of fellowship, I was invited to join the full-time faculty. Each faculty member had a research project, mine involved the Facial Nerve.

In 1962 while a resident at the Medical College of VA., Irving Blatt published a paper entitled, "Parotid Salivary Flow Predicts Prognosis in Bell's Palsy."

This was only a theory. I wanted to test the theory to predict the ideal timing for surgical treatment of patients with Bell's Palsy.

A clinical study that began as a resident was continued through the two years in the military and now at Washington University in St. Louis

I placed a micro tube into the submandibular salivary duct opening located in the floor of the mouth in patients with Bell's Palsy. Salivary flow was measured shortly after the onset of facial paralysis. I observed poor recovery of facial functions in patients with loss of salivary flow.

I operated on patients with Bell's Palsy who had loss of salivary flow. The initial results indicated the outcomes were more favorable in those operated compared to results in patients treated with steroids.

My clinical research changed from patient observations to animal experiments. My colleagues at Washington U. made this decision. The consensus was to prove the theory in the laboratory with animals and not in the OR with patients.

That year in the animal laboratory, I published three seminal articles. One study earned the coveted Mosher Award for working out the topographical anatomy of the facial nerve in the cat.

The second important contribution was the Maximal Stimulation Test. I collaborated with the Chairman of Neurology at Washington University, Professor Wm. Landau. We demonstrated in a controlled study in the animal lab that the number of nerve fibers surviving an injury could be determined. A maximum electrical stimulus caused the facial muscles to contract proportionately to the number of functioning nerve fibers. This observation was later confirmed in patients.

The third paper supported Blatt's theory that the reduction in volume of salivary flow correlated with the severity of facial nerve injury.

44)   Hugh Biller and Writing Skills

The year in the lab provided an opportunity to meet some of the superstars among the staff. Most were engaged in head and neck cancer research, Ogura's main interest.

Hugh Biller was Ogura's chosen one. He came to Washington U from Johns Hopkins in 1967, a year before I arrived. He was already recognized as a gifted surgeon, an exceptional teacher, and was well qualified to run Ogura's clinical service. Hugh was respected for his impeccable honesty and his willingness to share his unique qualities. He helped me to write papers intended for publication. Hugh was a genius with words. He had a knack of being able to condense a ten-page manuscript into two. Hugh was doctor "brevity and clarity". His shared writing skills were a major contribution to my success in publishing scientific articles.

Doctor Ogura required that he review all papers before submitted for publication. If he added his name as one of the authors, that was an indication of approval.

The first paper that I submitted to Dr. Ogura was over 20 pages. He picked up the manuscript that I thought was ready for publication and he flipped the pages like one shuffle a deck of cards. Without reading even one word, he handed it back to me, looked over his half frame reading glasses and said, "Bring it back with 5 pages." Biller worked his magic and Ogura accepted it.

After working with Ogura for four years, Hugh was recruited by Mt. Sinai Hospital in NYC. At the age of 37, he was the youngest chairman ever appointed at Mt. Sinai. He took over the ENT Department and under his leadership the program became one of the premier Otolaryngology/H & N Surgery Centers in the nation.

We remained friends and respected colleagues. Hugh invited me to his department as visiting professor on several occasions. He passed away February 22nd, 2015 at age 80.

45)   Harvey Tucker, My Best Friend

Harvey Tucker was another hard charger and even at over 80 years of age, continues working at MetroHealth in Cleveland.

He was appointed the National Institute of Health Head and Neck Cancer Fellow following my year as a fellow. Harvey was well trained from Jefferson Medical School in Philadelphia. Jefferson's department was strong in ENT endoscopy and laryngeal surgery.

As was the fate of all the H & N Fellows, Harvey was sent to the lab for a year of research. His lab project was a success. Harvey was the first to reinnervate a transplanted dog larynx. This was a major contribution to Ogura's transplant program.

After Harvey left the department, this break-through was applied to patients with a paralyzed vocal cord. The success of this procedure brought Harvey notoriety and patient referrals from all over the world. His administrative, writing, and teaching skills earned him the coveted chairmanship of the ENT Department at the Cleveland Clinic.

46)   Homer G. Phillips Hospital

Harvey, as a fellow, was an over achiever who yearned to apply his skills in the human realm.

Our lack of hands on experience because of the Department policy concerning "no touch" and "no surgery" of Ogura's patients was more than satisfied when we were assigned to care for a medically neglected population of indigent patients at Homer G Phillips Hospital. We worked with "Joe" West, a private ENT specialist who was the Chief of the service.

Harvey & I made teaching rounds every morning and evening, supervised surgery and dedicated most of our efforts training residents. The residents were all foreign trained. They were from India, Korea, Thailand and one Afro American.

Our efforts paid off. For the first time, the HGP ENT residents passed the Board Examinations of American Otolaryngology; that included all the graduating residents. Amnoy Cutchavaree became the Chairman of the ENT Department at Chulalongkorn Medical School in Bangkok and founder and editor of the first ENT Journal of Thailand.

HGP was understaffed and poorly supported financially. Key support depended on consultation with the staff of Washington University, the mother institution. Consultation was limited to telephone conferences. I don't remember a single instance of a surgical specialist from Washington U coming to HGP to perform surgery. This required that Harvey and I had to innovate and apply our surgical skills in the role of the other surgical subspecialties not readily available at HGP.

For example, we enucleated a damaged eye, removed a bullet from the neck that encroached on the spinal cord, or split a clavicle to control bleeding from a subclavian artery. Normally an ENT surgeon would call upon an ophthalmologic surgeon to remove an eye ball, a neurosurgeon to manage a bullet near the spinal cord and a vascular surgeon to repair the torn subclavian artery. We had no option; there was no time but to render life-saving emergency care.

We learned an important lesson when the neurosurgeon on call answered his phone at 4 AM. We pleaded, "Please come in and help us remove a bullet lodged against the cervical spine." We were astounded by his response. "Ask the OR nurse for the Neurosurgical tray, that's what I would do." He then hung up.

From then on, we identified the area of specialty and instead of calling the specialist; we called for his special instrument tray.

The challenge at HGP provided an ideal setting for Harvey and me to work as a team. There was a reservoir of patients with advanced head and neck cancer. Harvey and I took on the challenge to offer hope for the neglected. We performed major surgery, huge resections of cancerous tumors, and advanced reconstruction with major tissue flap transfers and bone grafts. Our overall success rate was higher than expected. Unlike cancer elsewhere in the body, head and neck cancer remains localized and often reaches a large size before spreading (metastasizing) to areas outside of the site of origin.

HGP earned the title of "America's Capital of Head and Neck Penetrating Wounds". Each weekend, five or more major head and neck trauma cases were brought to the ER. The doctors working in the HGP ER referred to the place as the "Busiest Knife and Gun Club West of the Mississippi".

I had some experience with penetrating wounds from my days in the ER at Hahnemann and during my residency in Richmond.

We documented our work with our Nikon cameras. The HGP residents were drilled to always take pictures first then call us.

In a short time, we accumulated pictures of clinical challenges never encountered by Dr. Ogura's elite staff. This became apparent at one of the Thursday Morning Weekly Department meetings. Eyes opened wide and mouths dropped as we presented our success stories.

Harvey & I didn't realize that the clinical challenges at HGP were so unusual. We were working in a "war zone" without realizing our situation.

47)   Knife and Gun Club

There was a reason the HGP ER was referred to as the "Knife and Gun Club". The "club" seemed to officially open for business at nightfall from Friday through Saturday. Over a six-year period, the club managed over 1000 penetrating head and neck wounds.

Many lessons were learned. Unlike high velocity military wounds that literally exploded upon entering the neck, low velocity civilian hand gun wounds can actually pass through and not cause any significant injury.

We discovered that all civilian head and neck penetrating wounds need not be explored. Providing large sized vessels, the trachea or esophagus were not penetrated exploration could be avoided.

A radiograph is indispensable to determine the course of the bullet and especially the depth and location of a knife. A bullet often leaves a lead fragment trail allowing one to trace the path.

In one case, the trail of lead fragments noted on the radiograph demonstrated that a penetrating wound can pass from one side of the neck and come out the other side without injuring any vital structure. He was treated with a tetanus shot, two band aids and discharged from the ER.

We learned the importance of ballistics and forensics and how to analyze wounds.

It was not unusual for a St. Louis Police Detective to accompany a shooting victim into the OR. On one occasion, we were told not to use forceps to remove the bullet and not to drop the bullet into a pan as depicted in the movies. The bullet is evidence. The markings can help identify the gun and ultimately single out the shooter. The markings on the bullet can be altered by the surgical forceps or by striking the pan.

We learned to recognize the caliber of the gun by the size of the wound. The most common wound encountered at the "Gun Club" was caused by the Saturday Night Special, an inexpensive .22 caliber hand gun.

The .22 had a street value of less than 100 dollars, rarely shot straight and usually was not lethal. At least that was our experience; we didn't see the fatal wounds.

The larger caliber guns like a .32, .38 and .45 were used by more serious shooters; the higher caliber guns were used by police and professional hit men working for the drug mob.

Multiple low caliber gun- shot wounds, especially to the groin area were associated with revenge for unfaithfulness. A lethal shot to the head suggests a professional hit. Our experience indicated that women prefer a knife over a gun and the location of the wound suggested the motive.

We managed several shot gun wounds (SGW). The blast of pellets and wadding at close range causes a large deep wound with disruption of skin and underlying bone. This required special management; wound debridement to remove the large number of foreign objects and leaving the wound packed with medicated gauze for ten days to three weeks before efforts to start reconstruction.

A lady was accidentally shot at close range. A life saving tracheotomy was performed in the ER. In the OR the wound was debrided, the distal ends of the facial nerve were identified with a nerve stimulator and tagged with a blue colored nylon suture for later identification and repair.

One year later, the large gaping wound healed with acceptable scaring and facial movement that provided tone , symmetry, a smile and weak eye closure.

48)   Axe in the Eye

A middle- aged woman was brought to the ER in a police van. She was covered in fresh blood and screaming unintelligibly. The nurses sprang into action. They cut off all of her clothes searching for the site of bleeding. None was found. Finally, her screams became coherent. "I killed him, I killed him!"

The police returned to her apartment and found her male partner in a drunken stupor. The full story unfolded. He came home and discovered the unopened welfare check. He purchased a liter of cheap wine and drank the whole bottle.

Prior to being brought into the ER, the woman had come home and realized that her welfare check was stolen. She became so angry that she took an axe, stood over her drunken partner and brought the axe down across his head.

He never woke up. She tried to revive him and failed. She was convinced that she had killed him. She was trying to tell us what happened and the blood was his.

He woke up in the ER, quite alive with the axe still in place, imbedded in his forehead and extending into his left eye. A radiograph showed the axe never entered the intracranial space, sparing his brain. The axe was removed, facial bones were repaired and the lacerated soft tissue was sutured back in place. The eye could not be saved. This was my first eye enucleation.

49)   Elevator Hold Up

A night in the OR removing bullets was exhausting. After 18 hours without sleep, I headed down on the elevator to the parking lot. Before reaching the parking level, I felt a sharp object poking me in my back.

I reached behind and encountered a knife.

"Don't turn around and give me your money." Foolishly, I did turn around and recognized my assailant.

"What are you doing? I am the doctor who just saved your brother's life!" I exclaimed. "Sorry, Doc!" He said and escorted me safely to my car.

My friend Harvey, after having been robbed on one occasion while in Philadelphia, "packed" a .38 caliber Police Special Snub Nose 5 shot manufactured in Brazil. He always carried his gun whenever he was called to HGP at night. The criminal element must have known as Harvey was never confronted.

Chapter 6

Medical Students

50)   An Addicted Teacher

So far, the stories in chapter 5 demonstrated how I dealt with adversities in a high-powered academic environment. I became an OR photographer to gain entrance to surgeries. Exile to the animal laboratory became a time for discovery. At HGP, I teamed up with Harvey Tucker to make a failing ENT training program into one that was successful. The next challenge was earning the respect of disgruntled senior medical students.

In July of 1969, shortly after my appointment to the full- time staff, I was summoned to Dr. Ogura's office. He showed me a letter from the dean. The medical school graduating class for the third consecutive year found that the Department of Otolaryngology was the worst department for teaching. As a result, the dean placed the ENT Department on probation.

Ogura said, "May, you are now the department's Medical Student Coordinator of Education."

I received a badge with my new title and a small office with a sign indicating my new role.

I inquired, "How will I find a medical student?" "Don't worry, they will find you."

The next day two senior medical students showed up unannounced, both wearing short white coats, their pockets filled with small manuals and a stethoscope draped around their neck. We exchanged some small talk as an introduction and then made our way to the ENT clinic.

We had a great first day learning how to examine the ear, nose and throat. I informed them to practice learning by examining each other. This required tolerating pain as their partner shoved a rigid instrument into their sensitive ear canal, suppressing the gag reflex provoked by a wooden stick placed on top of the back of their tongue and a reflecting mirror pushed against the soft palate. Their inexperience caused gagging, even retching, and created great discomfort and pain. This was one of the reasons medical students have so much trouble learning the skills required to examine the structures of the head and neck.

To put an end to this torture, I volunteered my body. This way, I could give them immediate feed-back and "gently" direct instruments into the proper orifices. I discovered that I had decreased sensation from my palate to my esophagus and almost no gag reflex. I turned out to the perfect living mannequin for them to practice on. This act of martyrdom won their respect.

Medical students who elected ENT were adopted by me and taken with me wherever my duties required. They went to the lab, HGP and to the clinic. They loved the attention and I loved their zeal for learning. It was at that moment I became an addicted teacher.

51)   Fat Jack

Shortly after becoming the Medical Student Coordinator, the Wash. U. ENT Department received a request from the state funded program for hearing impaired children.

"Is it possible for you to send an ENT doctor and audiologist to evaluate our hearing-impaired children who reside in the southeastern part of Missouri?"

The request was passed on to me to organize. My contact person was Mrs. Rosanna Herzog, the Public Health Nurse who resided in St. Genevieve, Mo. After a conversation with Rosanna, I agreed to visit St. Genevieve. I took the two students and Sue Ellen Fredman, an audiologist from our Department and drove an hour down federal highway 55 to St. Genevieve Memorial Hospital. Our first clinic was held in the hospital auditorium.

I discovered that there were no ENT specialists south of St. Louis. Children suspected of hearing loss were referred to Fat Jack, the "Hearing Aid Dealer". All children with a 20 percent or more hearing loss were fitted with a hearing aid regardless of cause. The State of Missouri reimbursed Fat Jack for all hearing aids, no questions asked.

At our first clinic, six children were evaluated. They all wore Fat Jack's hearing aids. The findings were striking. A 10-year-old was wearing bilateral aids for two years. The aids were removed and impacted ear wax was washed out. The ear drum on both sides appeared normal. Normal hearing detected in response to tuning fork testing was confirmed by a complete hearing test performed by Sue Ellen, the University audiologist.

One child had a congenital (from birth) hearing loss and would benefit from a more powerful (body) aid along with remedial education like lip reading. Four children had surgically correctable disorders. Two with middle ear fluid, residual from a URI, could be cured with a simple opening in the tympanic membrane (TM). Another had middle ear fluid but was associated with obstructive chronically infected tonsils and adenoids. This condition was associated with not only hearing loss but also foul-smelling breath and difficulty breathing at night. I recommended removal of the tonsils and adenoids in addition to opening and draining the fluid from the middle ear.

The last child had a potentially destructive and life-threatening disorder referred to as a Cholesteatoma (in-growth of infected skin from a hole on the TM).

Everyone present at the first clinic was impressed with our findings. That was all except Fat Jack, the "Hearing Aid Man". He showed up at the lunch break. He was a business man and tried to salvage his business that he had with the state reimbursement arrangement. Clearly, he had fitted some children with hearing aids that didn't qualify medically. As a hearing aid dealer, he had no medical training and couldn't be held responsible for his lack of diagnostic acumen. We met and I reassured him, now with an ENT consultant and a board-certified audiologist, more children would be found eligible for his services than before.

These clinics grew in popularity. We were invited back by the Public Health Service on a regular basis. At first every six weeks until other regions of SE Missouri requested that we come to their area as well. We held clinics in Perrysville, Fredericktown and Cape Girardeau. The frequency increased from every 6 weeks to every 3. The patient population grew from 6 school children to 20. Adults began to come as well. This service was convenient and free.

Fat Jack became an integral part of this project. He provided a pizza lunch and cold drinks for the volunteer staff. The medical students considered this a real treat; they loved pizza.

Fat Jack was so grateful that his business increased, as I predicted. He pulled me aside and asked if I would like to see a picture of his friend with the largest neck mass ever photographed. I gathered round the students to see this medical wonder. Fat Jack made us all swear to secrecy and not to publish the photo he was about to show us for at least 50 years. Now, we were all highly curious. Out of an 8 ½ by 11 manila envelope, Fat Jack removed the photo.

Fat Jack's friend hid this mass under his shirt. It started as a bump on his neck just below the jaw line and, over many years, got bigger and bigger. He was told not to disturb it or risk bleeding to death.

This was the largest neck mass that I ever encountered. It must have weighed at least fifty pounds. I pointed out to the students that this represented an example of the advantage of choosing ENT as a specialty. This case demonstrated that in ENT, a diagnosis can be made with just a glance. No history, physical examination, lab tests or imaging studies were required. This was an obstructed sebaceous skin gland that got bigger and bigger, and heavier and heavier. Over the years it had developed into gigantic benign neck mass.

I told the students, "This giant tumor could be removed as an office outpatient procedure with an Electrocautery, curette, tweezers and scissors, without blood loss or sutures."

The next day, I showed them a video made of me removing a giant sebaceous tumor from the scalp of a patient using the approach described.

These clinics were ideal for medical students. We transported them, fed them and treated them like practicing doctors. The clinics were set up so that each student had their own station in the auditorium to evaluate a patient assigned to them. When they completed their evaluation, I would visit each station with the entire staff and go over the findings. After each overview evaluation, the diagnosis was confirmed and treatment outlined. The word got out among the medical students and ENT became the most popular elective.

52)   Marriage Consummation

The medical students loved diagnostic mysteries or "Who Done It" cases. A medical student evaluated a newly married woman with a strange and baffling complaint. She claimed that she was unable to breathe lying on her back. This presented a challenge for her marital obligations.

She received no medical relief after consulting with a number of local "docs". She was treated for sinusitis with antibiotics, decongestants and steroid sprays, months of allergic therapy and even C-PAP, an approach for sleep apnea.

I stressed to the students that the most important clue was the chief complaint and next was looking and listening. Invariably, the patient will tell you the diagnosis. Once you know the cause, the treatment can be found in the textbook, but you must know the diagnosis to find the treatment.

We all gathered round to unravel this mystery. "First, let us employ the observations of a discerning eye." There was a slight suggestion of a runny nose, redness around the nostrils and occasional sniffing. Her voice was that of someone with nasal obstruction as if she had a cold (URI). Her mouth was dry and remained open. These observations supported her admission that she was unable to breathe through her nose.

We discussed the differential diagnosis of these signs. I intentionally provoked their thought processes. They listed URI, allergy, sinusitis and nasal foreign body obstructing the nasal passageway.

We considered each of these common disorders. "OK, let us look into the nose."

Both nasal passages were filled with thick clear odorless mucoid secretions. This ruled out foreign body that would obstruct one side and not the other. Allergy causes clear watery drainage and the discharge from chronic sinusitis would be malodorous and yellowish.

"Would you like to ask the patient any questions or look in any other ENT area?" Rather than prolong the process, I led them to the site of obstruction. "Look over my shoulder."

My headlight illuminated the oral cavity for all to see. A tongue blade depressed the tongue bringing the soft palate into view. "Note how the palate is pushed forward into the mouth and a smooth opaque mass makes an appearance along the leading edge of the palate."

The student who initially examined this patient missed this obvious sign. I didn't say anything to embarrass him. The Washington University students were among the highest academic achievers in the country.

The sign was missed not because he didn't see it but because he didn't recognize its significance. This was the first time he had ever seen a mass hanging down from behind the nose and pushing the palate forward. Those present will never miss this sign again.

The mass represented either an Angiofibroma or an Antral Choanal Polyp. An Angiofibroma usually occurs in young males and is accompanied by a history of recurrent nose bleeds. In addition an Angiofibroma appears highly vascular. I pointed out that our patient's complaint was most likely due to an Antral-Choanal Polyp; she was a 30 plus year old woman, no history of nose bleeds and the mass was pale and reflective.

This patient's marital issues were solved by removing a large Antral-Choanal Polyp. Six weeks later, at the follow-up clinic in St. Genevieve, the patient was free of symptoms and her facial expression reflected her gratitude.

53)

Cough and the Cocklebur

A teenage boy complained of a chronic cough present for six months. He was evaluated at the Cape Girardeau Health Clinic by a Washington University student. The assigned student was baffled. I discussed the differential diagnosis of chronic cough. The list included tuberculosis to a hair in the ear. This recitation was always impressive but rarely productive. Lung cancer is high on the list if the patient was an adult smoker, while bronchiectasis or abscess must be considered if the sputum is copious and purulent (dark brown and foul smelling).

A localized whistle or wheeze on inspiration or expiration suggested a foreign body or asthma even with a normal chest radiograph.

Prior to his evaluation at our clinic, he was admitted to the University Pulmonary (lung) service. After a week of tests, he was discharged without a definitive diagnosis. The discharge report read: "Rule out, irritative cough syndrome, nervous cough reflex and post viral chronic cough syndrome." Basically, the diagnosis remained a mystery.

He didn't have a hair lodged against his ear drum but he did have a whistle detected. Upon expiration, we could hear the abnormal sound by placing a stethoscope over the right nipple area.

A bronchoscopy (direct view of the trachea and bronchial tubes) was not performed while on the University service. I emphasized to the students that the evaluation in a case like this was incomplete without a bronchoscopy.

The students were all present when I performed the bronchoscopy and pulled out an infected cocklebur wedged into the teenager's right main stem bronchus. After he recovered from the anesthetic, miraculously his cough was gone. We showed him the bur. He immediately recalled running through the field on his way home from school. A bur was attached to his glove. He grasped it with his teeth and accidentally inhaled it.

These spectacular cases impressed the medical students as well as the rest of those attending the clinics. I tried to put things in perspective in order to play down this hero image. I stressed that everyone can improve their diagnostic skills by applying the following principles:

1) There is always a cause; it is up to us to find it.

2) Diagnosis requires remembering the "Rail Road Crossing Sign" ... Stop, Look and Listen to the patient.

3) Take the bag off of the patient's head... look into all the orifices. You must be able to examine the ENT structures.

54)   GI Bleed, Toe to Tonsil

After several months as the student coordinator for the Department of Otolaryngology, the teaching clinics in SW Missouri (with the help of Fat Jack's pizza and lots of love), seventy percent of the seniors clamored to sign up for ENT. Ogura noted an increase in resident applications from Washington University students.

The students were convinced that I could solve all diagnostic dilemmas, and consultation requests from the Medical Service began to appear.

There were two cases of note that clinched the basis for my legend. Both involved GI bleeding. The first patient was the most spectacular. The students put in a request for my input because I stressed there was always a cause; our job was to find it. Until that moment the proper treatment was a guess and delay could be fatal.

A 35 year old man was admitted from the ER to the medical service. He was severely anemic from chronic blood loss. His stools were black, a sign that he was bleeding internally from somewhere in his digestive tract. He required four bottles of blood to restore his blood pressure and pulse back to the low normal range. The location of the bleeding went undetected after a week of testing.

When I arrived at the patient's room, there was no way for me to get close enough to check for ENT abnormalities. The place was packed with suits (attendings), long and short white coats (residents and students respectively).

Instead of pushing my way into the crowd, I reviewed the chart hanging in a rack at the nurses' station. This patient had been checked by almost every medical specialist in the fields of bleeding disorders to tropical diseases. The nurse told me this crowd scene goes on every day, morning and afternoon.

The notes written by the multiple consultants were long and detailed. In spite of the length and detail, no one had a clue as to the cause or location of this patients bleeding.

I approached the doorway of the crowded room. Unbelievable, I thought. Through the break in the suits and white coats, I got a glimpse of the patient's right big toe. The sheet got pulled up and there it was.

The student who requested the consultation was anxious to read my note. I wrote, "OWR."

I signed my name and retreated to Barnes, the ENT Hospital where I was more comfortable. The attending called me, "What does OWR mean?" I told him, "OWR stands for Osler Weber Rendu Syndrome." I added, "There was a red spot on the right big toe. This is a telangectasia and part of the syndrome OWR, or Familial, Hemorrhagic Telangectasia. The most common site of bleeding is from the nasal septum."

Fortunately for me, I was correct and my legend was preserved. I suppose the medical staff were either impressed or tried to discredit me. One never knows. A week later I was called again for a similar case of occult GI bleeding. Occult is a medical term that means unknown or undetected.

In this case, the diagnosis was established with a pen light and tongue blade. For an ENT specialist any lesion that is visible can be diagnosed. This patient had a bleeding ulcerated tonsil cancer located on the right tongue base. It was cured by radiation therapy.

55)   Teacher of the Year

That year, the graduating class chose the ENT department as the best teaching service and yours truly as the Teacher of the Year.

At this point, I must caution the reader that I, Dr. Mark May, am not a super doctor but one who has failures like everyone else. As an example, I will share one story. A 60ish man complained of difficulty breathing. He had an obvious scar on top of his crooked nose. He related that as a young boy, he was struck across his nose with a shovel by his older brother. An examination of his nose revealed a severe septal deviation obstructing breathing. Nasal surgery was performed. The crooked nasal septum was straightened. Within days after the surgery, he was grateful to be able to breathe through his nose.

Three weeks later his internist and a frequent source of referrals called me. I was certain it was to thank me for the excellent care of his patient.

"The patient has been hospitalized. He is in room 518. He was admitted today with congestive heart failure. Next time you schedule a patient for a nose job, check for ankle swelling (a sign of congestive heart failure). "

Humility is a virtue that requires reminders. It is not possible to practice medicine and not have constant reminders that we just work here like everybody else.

Chapter 7

Private Practice

56)   <u>Decision to go Private</u>

As I reflect on my life as a doctor, the first 14 years started as a medical student and ended as a full time academic. I was primarily working as a volunteer. I could have joined the U.S. Public Health Service, organizations like Doctors without Borders, moved to an American Indian Reservation or trekked through the dense jungles of the Congo and worked as the village doctor. During my years of service, I made the best of my assignment but was never in control.

My experience managing trauma in the "war zone" at the emergency rooms of Hahnemann, MCV and HGP Hospital involved caring for the poor, forgotten and downtrodden. In spite of my dedication, there was never an opportunity to develop long term relationships. After an exciting night performing heroic surgery on "John Doe", he remained a body and never a person with a name and a family.

I will never forget the drunken guy with a severe nose bleed. I responded to a 3 am call from the ER. He was obnoxious and uncooperative. He spat his blood all over me and regurgitated his belly full of smelly beer and undigested sausage that covered the ER floor and the tops of my shoes. It could have been worse. I had no choice but to leave him with his nose still bleeding when he shared his crude vocabulary of expletives directed at me. Those of us who worked in this environment, had an expression that applied to cases like this one, "All bleeding stops eventually."

On another occasion, I received an ER distress call. It was late at night, well past my bedtime. Take my word, it was not fun to leave a warm bed to meet a gorilla chained to a gurney with three police officers taking turns beating the guy with their Billy clubs each time he cursed them. The guy had deep lacerations across his forehead and a cheek that needed to be sutured. I prepared the prisoner, wiped the wounds with disinfectant, and covered his face with a sterile sheet that had a hole exposing the wounds. The nurse brought over a suture tray. I told the patient under the sheet that I am a doctor and I will try not to hurt him. I started to inject the local. As soon as the needle touched the edge of his wound, the gorilla went into a rage and the instruments went flying. It scared the heebie jeebies out of me. The police dragged him off to jail with his open wounds. Is it any wonder that after that experience, I couldn't fall asleep the rest of that night?

My turn off was the drunks, the filthy bodies, and gutter language. The cruelty and senseless inhumanities of barbarians using knives, axes and guns to maim or murder each other, most of the time for no reason.

On the positive side, this unique experience prepared me to manage trauma victims encountered in private practice.

Facial Nerve

My sustained interest in facial nerve disorders was ignited while a resident caring for the librarian, a young lady who faithfully came to the clinic for her care (Story #28).

My academic career allowed me to meet the leaders in the field of facial nerve disorders. I will never forget when John Conley, one of the world leaders in Facial Reanimation, joined my wife and me for breakfast while attending the 1976 International Facial Nerve Symposium held in Zurich, Switzerland.
He said, "Mark, I was impressed with the number of patients that you have studied with facial paralysis; you reported 150 or so. If I saw that many patients with facial paralysis, I sure would design a surgical procedure to help restore their smile."

At that meeting there was an explosion of new operations presented including the cross-face graft, free muscle nerve transfers, 12-7 and 5-7 hook ups, the temporalis muscle transposition, approaches for reanimating the paralyzed eyelids

and so much more. I came home from that meeting all fired up.
Ten years later, in 1986, I wrote the first edition of the Facial
Nerve Book. In 1996, Barry Schaitkin helped me publish the
revised edition.

Pittsburgh

The move to Pittsburgh in 1974 was the start of 22 years of
private practice and offered an opportunity to continue
teaching, pursue laboratory and clinical research.

In Pittsburgh, there was an old friend and colleague, Gene
Myers. He graduated Central High School one year ahead of me.
Gene's dad, Dave Myers, was a famous ear surgeon known for
treating otosclerosis with a procedure called a Stapedectomy.
The operation was done under local anesthesia and was highly
successful in restoring hearing. Dave Myers operated on three
members of my mother's side of the family; otosclerosis
frequently involves family members. While I was a senior
medical student at Hahnemann, Dave Myers presented his
surgical experience. This presentation was a positive influence
that encouraged me to choose ENT as a specialty.

It was probably not a coincidence that I would reconnect with
the Myers'. One year before I arrived, Gene Myers was
appointed chairman of the ENT department at the U. of

Pittsburgh. When he learned that I decided to relocate, he offered me a position as a member of his fulltime staff. He provided me with an office and encouraged me to teach the residents and medical students. I was awarded Outstanding Teacher after my second year.

Gene tried to persuade me to join his department; I expressed my appreciation for the offer. During our conversation, I reminded Gene how we both applied for Ogura's NIH Fellowship Program and I was chosen. Did you ever wonder why Ogura chose me over you? Your credentials were far more impressive than mine.

I related what Ogura had told me; my application for Ogura's Fellowship was addressed to John Conley and my application for Ogura's program went to Conley. Ogura took notice and thought, I'll be damned if I'll allow Conley to take this top candidate from me.

I thought it was ironic that Gene was appointed to department chairman after a fellowship with Conley. Conley's fellows rarely became Department Chairmen. I spent six years with Ogura preparing for a career in academics and yet chose private practice.

I explained to Gene that full time was not for me. I needed to be independent and I didn't fare well on someone else's leash.

For example, while working for Ogura, I was approved to go to Nasau in the Bahamas for the Eastern Sectional Meeting. I presented my paper on the first day; the rest of the week bad weather was predicted. I arranged to travel to New Orleans where the Southern Section was meeting. Ogura spotted me walking out of the Nasau Hotel with my wife and our bags.

"May! Where are you going?" He called after me. I told him my plan and he responded, "If you go to New Orleans, you go on your own nickel."

Even though there were no additional expenses, that moment was an embarrassing one for me.

A major issue for me recurred throughout my academic career. I had no control of my life. I applied for funds for a camera to fit on the operating microscope as a teaching aid. This request had to go through a committee with Ogura's final approval. The funds in this case were awarded to me by the dean in recognition for the Teacher of the Year Award. The funds were to be spent at my discretion providing the funds were used for teaching. Ogura made it clear to me that those funds belonged to his department.

Ogura refurbished his spacious office costing thousands of dollars, thick rugs, surround sound and leather covered furniture. He had two secretaries, flew first class, and we served him as if he was the king.

As a member of his department, my office was big enough for one small desk and two plain chairs covered with plastic. On my desk was a green shaded night lamp, and against the free wall was a table with cages containing my experimental rats infected with herpes virus. We were given a $100 gift certificate to use to "beautify" our office. I purchased a wall sized mural poster of Half Dome found in Yosemite National Park. I hung it up with masking tape. It covered three walls leaving one wall bare. This one wall had a window that could not be opened and allowed no light to enter my cave. My "office" had no natural light and no ventilation. I didn't cover this wall with the window hoping Ogura would approve opening it and installing an air conditioner. He never did.

The breaking point that convinced me to leave academics and give up the promise that one day I would be king like Ogura, occurred in May of 1974. Ogura took me on a personal tour showing me the blue prints of his new physical plant, his dream facility that included constructing a bridge from his office to the University building. We did a walk around. I felt like a big shot chosen by the boss as a confidant. Ogura made me think that I was his number one.

At that time, I had every intention to remain fulltime. Ogura promised me a large space for my planned "taste and smell" clinic. He showed me on the blueprint the location that would be mine. The next day, I rechecked the blue prints to write down the dimensions. I wanted to sketch in how to arrange the reception area, the patient examining rooms, and research space. When I got close, I read the label for this designated area. In fine print it said: broom closet.

Group Private Practice

One month later, while as the invited guest speaker at the Annual Pennsylvania Academy ENT Society meeting, I met Herman Felder. He was a successful private ENT doctor practicing in Pittsburgh. He was looking for an associate who would join him. Buddy Bluestone was his partner who left to pursue an academic position at Boston Children's Hospital as a Pediatric Otolaryngologist.

Herman Felder's offer for a new associate seemed generous. After consulting with my wife, I accepted. I worked with Herman and his other associate, Joe Zahorchak, from 1974 to November 1980. Herman's main interest was treating children and Joe was an accomplished rhinoplasty surgeon.

After five and half years, I realized that I needed to go out on my own. My special requirements needed to be addressed. My partners kept their patient records on index cards and I wrote my long and detailed notes on 8 1/2 x 11 sized lined papers. This, in turn, demanded purchasing larger filing storage cabinets. I needed a minimum of twenty minutes or longer to evaluate a new patient compared to Herman who had a five minute policy; either you talk or he does, but after five minutes the visit was over.

The office had one binocular microscope shared by the three of us. They monopolized the scope checking the status of their pre-op or post-op myringotomy patients. This was ninety percent of their practice.

I attended every major National ENT meeting and was away from the office a half a dozen times per year attending State ENT Society meetings as an invited guest speaker or panelist.

Upon my return, I was reminded that when away from the office, there was no income. I was never asked to share what I learned. It was clear that my practice was incompatible with Herman's; I needed to be on my own.

<u>Solo Private Practice</u>

In January 1981, I rented space above George Aiken Fried Chicken, a take-out restaurant located across the street and up the block from Felder's office.

I remember our expendable income was limited. I purchased a binocular microscope designed for office use, one mechanical chair, one ENT examining consul, three nasal speculae, one set of ear speculae , four wire cotton applicators and cotton balls, one otoscope, three reflecting mirrors to examine the patient's vocal cords, a sound proof booth, an audiometer to test hearing and a set of ten inexpensive chairs for the waiting room. The Storz instrument company extended me a $100,000 advance without interest.

I remember driving to the air cargo terminal at the Pittsburgh International Airport on a snowy day in January. I was so excited to load the new ENT equipment into a rented van and deliver it to our new office in time for opening day; my first day as a solo-practitioner.

We hired an amateur carpenter because the price was right. He built a counter where patients registered and some shelving to store supplies. All the table tops had a slant. This was remedied by using only square pencils.

My wife learned how to be the business manager. It took her one month to master the job. Our personnel included Roz Solomon as secretary and Susan Klein as the audiologist. The job offer had a condition, no pay check until we received our first payment from the insurance companies; there was an average of six weeks between service and payment. They were both paid on time during their entire 15 years of employment.

My practice grew slowly; Pittsburgh had a high concentration of ENT doctors. I discovered that all my previous academic achievements, awards, degrees, honors and accolades meant nothing. In private practice, it is rare that a competing colleague will refer to another competitor. Either the referral went to Gene Myers or to an out of town doctor. That was just the way it was and will always be.

It would take me five years to build a patient referral base. Today, patients go where their insurance company dictates or to large clinics or hospital complexes that actively market with billboards, radio ads, TV info-commercials or cleverly designed web-sites.

Henry Mordoh and Shadyside Hospital

In 1986, I was recruited by Henry Mordoh, CEO of Shadyside Hospital and David Zorub, Neurosurgeon and Chairman of the Medical Staff at Shadyside Hospital. At Shadyside Hospital there was vision; they stressed quality of care over cost. For the first time since I graduated from medical school, the bit was removed from my mouth; I was given space, support, funds and the latest equipment.

Working at the Eye and Ear Hospital of Pittsburgh, I was performing sophisticated facial nerve reanimation with a primitive microscope that depended on a low wattage dim incandescent bulb. I requested an upgrade. A committee ruled that my request was granted but not approved for this year's budget due to insufficient funds. The committee's recommendation was to reapply for next year's budget. I protested and was told, "Why do you have to be different, no one else complains about the microscope except you. Your problem is that you think you're special."

I countered, "How many on the staff at E & E repair facial nerves?!"

Sinus Surgery
_____

The move to Shadyside Hospital was a dream come true. I had a major shift in my area of interest, managing sinus disorders using the endonasal endoscopic approach.

It started in 1985, the year before I relocated to Shadyside Hospital. I met Heinz Stammberger, a visiting doctor from Graz, Austria. He was invited by Sylvan Stool, a University of Pittsburgh Pediatric Otolaryngologist. Stammberger demonstrated the optics of the Karl Storz manufactured Hopkins solid rod system. The hour program took place in Children's Hospital Auditorium. There were two others present besides me; Sylvan and Ed Elmer, a private ENT doctor. I was impressed with the clarity and depth of field and particularly the wide angled view provided by this system.

At that time, enthusiasm for the endoscopic approach was dampened by most academics. The capital expense for the endoscopic equipment was a major limiting factor. The vast majority of those working in the universities resisted replacing traditional approaches with new concepts. So, often, there was a tendency to promote fads that fizzle. Gene Myers was one of those who could accomplish sinus surgery with a headlight, a nasal speculum and a grasping cup forceps. This strong position kept endoscopes out of Eye and Ear Hospital well into the 90s.

In 1986, as part of my signing contract, Henry Mordoh agreed to purchase a quarter of a million dollars worth of equipment. He satisfied my wish list with the latest fiber-optic illuminated binocular operating microscope with a high definition video camera attached. This was in striking contrast to the light bulb upgrade offered by E & E Hospital.

The package included sinus endoscopic instruments for the operating room (OR) and my private office. Recently, I checked with Michael Pivar, the sales representative for the Carl Storz Endoscope Company who sold us the equipment. He told me the invoice totaled $30,000 for my office and $50,000 for the OR.

Michael Pivar was instrumental (excuse the pun) in launching my career as one of the first in the United States who performed endoscopic naso-sinus surgery using the "Four-Handed Technique"; a TV monitor substituted for the standard approach working directly through the endoscope.

This was a major advantage for teaching others (residents, fellows, and colleagues) who attended our post graduate courses. Most importantly, it allowed the surgeon to use two hands; one to affectively use the suction to keep the surgical field clear of blood and secretions and the other to manipulate the tissues. The assistant, looking through the TV monitor, used the same view as the surgeon. The assistant learned to direct the endoscope in the nasal cavity to maintain visualization of the operative field and had their other hand to irrigate blood and secretions. This kept the end of the endoscope and the surgical field clear. This technique allowed the surgeon to operate on more advanced cases.

The "Four- Handed Technique" was discovered, by chance, early in my experience. In 1986, I was working at Shadyside Hospital. At that time, The Messerklinger- Stamberger- Kennedy School (MSK) taught to operate directly through the endoscope with one student viewing the surgery through a side arm.

On this particular day there were visiting doctors who came to observe. The classical set up for the MSK approach malfunctioned. I placed a call to Mike Pivar and he arrived within 30 minutes with a backup system that required working off the TV monitor. He not only saved the day, but was responsible for introducing the "Four- Handed Technique".

Post-Graduate Education

The University refused to put out any seed money or provide space to allow me to schedule post-graduate courses. I made a proposal to Henry Mordoh for a cadaver course. I required $25,000 for seed money. The purchase of cadavers cost $350 each and we needed 30. Prior to the course, each cadaver needed to be scanned by CT in the radiology department. The course would have to reserve the main auditorium for one week and a large room off the auditorium had to be secured to store audiovisual support equipment and conduct cadaver dissections. Mordoh replied "Done".

In 1987, Howard Levine from Cleveland agreed to teach the first Endoscopic Sinus Surgery Cadaver Dissection Course sponsored by Shadyside Hospital. This course was given twice a year until 1999. In addition to these 22 courses, Shadyside Hospital sponsored five Annual Ski Meetings and two International Sinus Surgery Symposia. Howard Levine and I published a book on the subject.

My appetite to master surgery of the paranasal sinuses using the endonasal endoscopic approach was insatiable. I took advantage of every learning opportunity, and cadaver dissections. I spent hours with the radiologist Kevin O'Hara correlating CT findings with what I saw with an endoscope during the office exam both in the OR and PO.

I took courses given by James Zinreich, a pioneer in imaging the paranasal sinuses. He teamed up with David Kennedy. At the time, they were both Johns Hopkins faculty members. I attended lectures given by Kennedy and Stammberger and studied articles written by them. There was no question for me that these two men brought this major contribution to North America and beyond.

Reuben Setliff introduced me to the Microdebrider, an instrument that removes disease almost like using the PhotoShop App. He became a regular at our dissection courses. His delineation of anatomical landmarks during his cadaver dissection was impressive. Reuben was a master teacher to whom I am grateful for his willingness to share.

I worked with Steve Sobel (now in Decatur, Illinois) for six months. I have never encountered a more skillful surgeon in my life. He taught me surgery of the sphenoid sinus, the surgical landmarks and techniques as one would expect from a gifted surgeon.

Professor Wolfgang Draf from Fulda, Germany who passed away on October 24th, 2011, taught me how to manage frontal sinus disease using the endonasal route. He invited me to Germany to participate in a Sinus Surgery Course sponsored by his department. My wife & I had the pleasure of enjoying his warm hospitality and even an intimate dinner at his home.

Barry Schaitkin was my associate at Shadyside Hospital and we worked together to advance this area of specialty. Barry ran the cadaver courses and ski meetings for three years after my retirement. Since then, Barry sold the practice to the University and works as a fulltime faculty member.

57)   Doctors and Nurses

(Inspired by Elisheva, our granddaughter, the aspiring nurse).

I quickly learned to appreciate the nurse on my first day as an intern in the "war zone" of Hahnemann's Emergency Room located in center city Philadelphia. The ER nurse guided me through the life saving steps required to manage a patient with multiple injuries (Story # 14). She taught me how to place a variety of tubes in every orifice, draw blood for tests, transfuse blood, select the proper medications to inject into an IV, make a cast for a fractured wrist, apply an arm sling and dress a burn wound all on my first day in the "war zone". I thought to myself, maybe I should have gone to nursing school.

My first encounter with the kindness of a nurse occurred the night I tried to prepare for my first time ever as a surgical assistant in the operating room (Story # 13). After cleaning my nails and scrubbing my hands and arms up to my elbows with an abrasive steel wool brush for the required five minutes, I backed into the swinging doors to enter the operating room.

The surgeon was grumbling, "Where is May?" I was perspiring and my nervous system was on high alert as I extended my hands for the nurse to dry and glove them. As I shoved my right hand into the glove, the glove tore and I contaminated the nurse. We both had to return to the torture involved in the rescrub.

I expected a scold and stern reprimand from the nurse. Instead, in a quiet soothing tone, I got comfort and reassurance. "It's OK, don't worry. This has happened to all of us. A one-minute scrub will be just fine."

The Army Nurse at Darnell Army Hospital in Killeen Texas was another breed (Chapter 4, Stories # 37-40). It took me six months until I proved worthy of working as a surgical colleague in her protected inner sanctum.

At first all my requests for more OR time or special equipment were met with, "May, you keep this up and you will receive your papers to ship out to Vietnam. Did you hear me? Vietnam, there is a war going on."

Following some spectacular surgical feats, things changed. OR time for ENT was expanded from one half day per week, to five full days. The OR upgraded the surgical instrumentation to accommodate Head and Neck as well as Otologic surgery. The days limiting ENT to only tonsils and adenoids were over. The nursing support supplemented with experienced corpsmen in the US military was excellent.

Stories # 60 & # 61 describe the reward for loving dedication. In the first story, #60, the nurse married the man whose life she saved. He was helicopter evacuated to the ER after an industrial explosion blew off half of his head. The ER doc pronounced him DOA (Dead on Arrival). The nurse noted a small spurtor from the scalp wound edge. He was successfully resuscitated and reconstructed. She cared for him during this entire process. They are happily married and raising a family.

The second story, #61 is similar. The girlfriend, a nurse, cared for her guy following a life-threatening facial deforming accident. After recovery they got married and are blessed with children.

The last 22 years of my career were spent in private practice. This period was unique for many reasons. One of the main elements was adding a private nurse to the team. A specialty surgeon is handicapped operating in most general hospitals. This is the rational to support specialty hospitals like an Eye and Ear Hospital or a hospital for Neurosurgery, Orthopedics, or Cardiac surgery. Each of these disciplines have special needs and require specially trained personal.

My life in the OR improved the day Judy Urso joined my team. She worked exclusively with me. I performed surgery with the aid of a binocular microscope which required total concentration. A camera was mounted on the microscope. This allowed Judy, the OR nurse, to follow the surgical procedure displayed on the video monitor. She anticipated the instrument I would need and had it ready when I put out my hand. I could tell by the feel whether that was the one needed, if not my hand stayed open and another instrument was placed. I never had to take my eyes away from the microscope.

Judy took care of my special instruments, cleaned them, sharpened them, and kept them locked away in our private tool chest (see story #20, Green Gloves). The private nurse was familiar with the patients, the diagnosis, operative procedures, and special needs. Judy became an integral and indispensable part of our smooth working team.

This dream team extended to the 7 West Section of Shadyside Hospital, a place for pre-op and post-op ENT patient care. This element of care was unique because of the dedication of the head nurse, Sue Martin, and her team of nurses. I personally taught them how to care for the special needs of an ENT patient. A tracheostomy tube had to be cleaned of mucus crusts by periodic gentle suctioning. A chest flap that becomes dusky required immediate attention. Relieving tension or loosening a tight dressing may preserve the viability of a chest flap. Leakage of spinal fluid will soak the dressing after naso-sinus or otologic surgery. The attending surgeon expected to be called without delay if any of these situations were recognized.

On 7 West there was a specialized evaluation and treatment room. This room contained everything required to support the special needs of ENT, an operating binocular microscope, suction, flexible and rigid endoscopes, topical decongestants and anesthetics.

A special relationship was established with the 7 West nursing staff. When I arrived at the nurses' desk each morning at 6 am, a nurse would have the charts of the ENT patients and would update me as we made quick rounds before I went to surgery. Once a week, I brought them either bagels and cream cheese or donuts; they provided the fresh coffee. We would schmooze and have a Q &A. We would discuss a problem patient or cover a topic of their interest. This session took about a half hour. They loved it. No other doctor on the staff gave them this attention. In my opinion, their devotion to my patients earned them this appreciation.

This special relationship had to be nurtured and had little tolerance for mistreatment. I discovered nurses are sensitive. On one occasion, one of my post-op patients was given a bowel softener that was intended for a patient on another service. The medicine was effective and the result was detected to my displeasure. Upon inquiry, I tracked down the culprit and let her know my feelings. I must have raised my voice and this was interpreted as scolding. The whole crew ganged up on me. I had to get on my knees and beg forgiveness. The standoff lasted until the following morning when my sentence ended. Two bags of treats helped; one with bagels and the other with donuts seemed to restore peace more than anything else.

I have fond memories working with nurses; the most dedicated members of the medical team. A nurse exudes kindness not only to patients but to the doctor as well. I will never forget the thoughtfulness of the OR circulating nurse, the dab with a gauze pad to blot my perspiring forehead or a straw connected to a cup of cold orange juice slipped under my surgical mask to quench my thirst. These thoughtful acts were provided by a nurse who empathized with the doctor who had been performing tedious surgery for several hours without a break.

There were humorous moments as well. Beulah was an old fashioned takeover Australian trained nurse. She was employed as a fulltime private nurse to work with me evaluating patients and scheduling surgery. She had strengths and shortcomings, both appreciated and tolerated.

Beulah always had my best interests in mind. She was known to screen patients in the waiting room and suggest how great I was and let the patient know that whatever the problem, Doctor May could solve it. She was a real confidence builder. I insisted that I see all patients that Beulah scheduled. The number of patients scheduled for cosmetic surgery increased. I discovered most made appointments for complaints unrelated to cosmetic concerns. Beulah explained that was how it worked with her previous ENT doctor. I gently explained that is not acceptable with me.

She was a skimper, scamping here and there. She needed more responsibility. I put her in charge of ordering supplies. We needed tongue blades. An ENT doc used lots of tongue blades, one for each patient. The ENT exam was incomplete without asking the patient to say, "Ahhh". This required a tongue blade to hold down the tongue.

Beulah found a special from a "going out of business" medical supply warehouse. She bought so many tongue blades, that every closet in our office was stacked with them. The fact is that Beulah over ordered tongue blades but the bargain price was impressive. Beulah was transferred from purchasing to sanitation officer. This job was key because I knew that if Beulah was in charge, we could be sure all of our equipment would be clean and sterile.

Beula retired when we moved our practice to Shadyside Hospital in '86. I retired ten years later and we still were using Beulah's tongue blades.

58)   Lou Frank Memorial Railroad

Shortly after arriving in Pittsburgh, I met Lou Frank. I vividly recall our first meeting. He was in his early 50s, heavy set with a short stature. He walked with the aid of a cane and wore dark rimmed eye glasses. His gray beard was full and untrimmed. He wore a tan flat newsboy type hat. His voice was gentle and he spoke with a slight slur. I learned that Lou suffered from the effects of multiple sclerosis. This explained the cane and slurred speech.

Lou complained of a growth in his mouth. Six years with Dr. Ogura evaluating head and neck cancer allowed me to diagnose the irregular wart like lesion as a verrucous carcinoma. The tumor was limited to the sulcus between the right gingiva and cheek. This commonly occurred in pipe smokers or tobacco chewers.

Lou's wife, Hilda, related that Lou was rarely without his lighted pipe clenched between his teeth hanging out of the right side of his mouth. Hilda, a school librarian, kept Lou in line and provided for his special needs. She added playfully with a loving smile that Lou was stubborn and incorrigible as well. Further, Lou refused to give up the pipe, claiming that it gave him so much pleasure.

They agreed to allow me to biopsy the growth. The diagnosis of verrucous carcinoma was confirmed. With their permission, the cancer was excised. The margins were clear and the long- term outcome was favorable.

Lou required follow-up visits every three months because verrucous carcinoma, although initially a local problem, tends to recur with patients like Lou; he continued smoking his pipe. Fortunately, Lou was a compliant patient and returned every three months for his check- up. I was able to control the frequent recurrences with local excisions.

I discovered that Lou, in addition to his regular employment as a chemist for the US Bureau of Mines, tinkered with carpentry and furniture refurbishing. He learned that my son Harry and I were building a model railroad in our basement and volunteered to help us.

Every Wednesday evening for 15 years, Harry and Lou Frank built a gigantic railroad. Lou referred to Harry as "boychik". Lou would place the nails and Harry hammered them in. It started with an 8-foot circle with one switch and ended with a layout 40 by 20 feet with a 20 by 7 foot dogleg extension.

We broke down brick walls in our basement, changed the electrical wiring, and moved sewage and water pipes. The railroad kept growing with 5 radio-controlled engines that ran at the same time over miles of track on three levels. It included an over and under bridge and a ski mountain with an operating gondola that took the skiers from the train depot to the top of the mountain. Running the railroad was complicated. There were 37 electronically controlled track switches. I was incapable of directing one engine around the complete layout without a crash. Only Harry could run five trains at the same time.

Lou Frank started as a patient and over the years he was embraced as a dear friend by our entire family.

After 15 years with railroad construction in progress, Lou did not show up for three weeks in a row. I called but there was no answer. I visited Lou at his home and found him sitting by the bedside with his wife Hilda who was dying of mesothelioma, an incurable fatal lung cancer caused by asbestos exposure. Asbestos is a filament-based installation used to cover steam pipes. The asbestos filaments could not be contained and escaped into the air. Hilda worked as a librarian in a local public school for twenty-five years. The school was condemned for asbestos exposure but never corrected.

Lou did not return for follow-up for an additional six months. Again, I visited Lou and was dismayed to find he had a far advanced mouth cancer. The cancer was fixed to deep neck structures and had reached an inoperable stage. I asked him

why he didn't keep his appointments and he explained that
Hilda died and he had no reason to go on living. Hilda was his
entire life. He described how Hilda took care of him after the
doctors diagnosed him with multiple sclerosis.

Two years later, Lou died from his cancer. Harry & I made a
video of our railroad built together with Lou. The video was
entitled <u>The Lou Frank Memorial Railroad</u>. The video awarded
to Lou's surviving family was much appreciated, especially by his
grandchildren, Eric and Jonathan.

59)   <u>Marijuana Leaf to Stop Bleeding</u>
Story as related by Dieter Hoffmann

The patient was a 50-year-old man who looked like he had just
gotten off a Harley Davidson. He sported long scraggly hair, a
patched jeans jacket, a pack of Marlboros protruding out of his
vest pocket, and multiple tattoos were visible on his neck and
arms. Despite his outward tough appearance, he was really a
pleasant guy. He presented with a skin fistula below his earlobe
that looked like a first branchial malformation. A branchial cleft
fistula was suspected by the location and appearance of the tiny
dimpled hole in the skin of his neck.

Branchial malformations are remnants of skin lining trapped
under the surface during embryonic formation during a phase

when the embryo resembles a fish. The branchial remnants are analogous to gills, and can be present during a person's lifetime as a cyst or a pitted hole in the skin leading to a tract of skin known as a fistula. A first branchial fistula can be closely associated with the facial nerve.

Treatment requires complete surgical removal with preservation of the facial nerve. Dr. Dieter Hoffman was in his last six months of his fellowship and transitioned to become my associate. At this point in his career, Dieter was an excellent surgeon with mature judgment. This was Dieter's case to manage.

He dissected the skin tract from the pit in the upper neck as it coursed through the parotid gland. A branchial skin fistula is soft and pliable; this lesion felt gritty and was stuck to the surrounding tissue. A malignancy was suspected and a biopsy was obtained. Hoffmann's suspicion was confirmed. The biopsy revealed squamous cell carcinoma.

Hoffmann wisely terminated the surgery; it was evident that a much larger procedure was necessary. Imaging was performed, and it appeared that the lesion could be successfully removed with a more radical procedure. Dieter explained to the patient that the procedure required would include removal of the parotid salivary gland, excision and grafting of the facial nerve, and a neck dissection.

The second surgery was performed several days later. The surgery included a neck dissection to remove cancer that might have spread to lymph nodes, resection of the entire parotid gland and the facial nerve along with a portion of the lower part of the external ear. In spite of this wide field resection, the deep margin was still too close to be certain that total removal of the cancer was achieved.

Dieter, upon my advice, drilled off the mastoid tip for a better margin. As the drilling progressed, Dr. H opened a hole in the jugular bulb, resulting in massive blood loss. Dr. H's shoes were soaked in the patient's blood; multiple units of blood replacement kept the patient stable. The jugular bulb is a large venous structure located within the base of the skull; blood from the brain drains through the bulb into the jugular vein in the neck. Because the jugular bulb is surrounded by bone and three cranial nerves, it is very difficult to suture or clamp.

Ultimately, the bleeding was controlled by packing Surgicel, a dissolvable material, into the jugular bulb along with over-suturing of local tissue.

The extensive wide field cancer operation created a deep defect that needed to be filled. Further, the packing into the jugular bulb was a temporary measure. We decided to use a chest flap to fill the defect and to cover the damaged jugular bulb.

A pectoralis skin-muscle flap from the upper chest was prepared. We noted that the patient sported a tattoo of a marijuana leaf covering the end of the flap; the part we needed to cover the jugular bulb area. The tattoo with skin and underlying chest muscle was rotated up to the patient's cheek and lower ear, where the tattoo took on a new position. The wound healed and the patient liked the new location of his tattoo!

This is the story of how a marijuana leaf was used to stop bleeding.

In this case, Doctor Hoffmann demonstrated sound judgment, the ability to respond in a crisis, and his versatility when challenged with the unexpected. These qualities were essential for a head and neck surgeon. I recognized that Dieter had these attributes. I tried to make him an attractive offer to work with me as an equal partner but he insisted that the lure of going west to ski and hike was much too great.

After fellowship, Dr. Hoffmann spent 30 years in Portland, Oregon at the Kaiser Permanente ENT department. Dieter distinguished himself as a gifted head and neck surgeon. He excelled in the areas he learned during his fellowship; facial nerve disorders, endoscopic sinus surgery and facial plastic surgery.

He and his wife Lynne raised 3 daughters, all of whom work in the medical field.

Recently, Dieter and his wife Lynn visited me in Israel. He related that I would pick him up in the morning at 6 am and bring him back home at the end of a working day. One morning after working past midnight the night before I asked him, "Tell me Dieter, what journal did you read last night?"

My wife always reminded me, "If you want to be a crazy workaholic, don't expect the normal people that work with you to be crazy too."

60)   In the Bag

Jim, a tall, handsome, and fit 28- year- old, who was a recent graduate from the West Virginia School of Mines, worked as an engineer for Phillips Petroleum Company. He was out in the hills of West Virginia with a team measuring the natural gas well head pressures. Just as he approached his target, there was a boom! The valve gasket exploded and metal projectiles struck Jim in the left side of his head. He was thrown to the ground and moments later his teammates found him unresponsive lying in a pool of blood with half his head blown off and brain tissue exposed.

A company helicopter was summoned and within 10 minutes Jim was taken to a local hospital ER. He was pronounced dead on arrival. He was put in a body bag and as the bag was zipped shut, the young blond ER nurse noted a vessel along the edge of the scalp wound was bleeding, actually pulsating. She screamed with excitement, "He is alive!"

Emergency resuscitative measures literally brought him back to life, thanks to the astute observation of the ER nurse. A Neurosurgeon debrided the damaged brain tissue and later closed the skull defect with a fabricated acrylic plate. The torn apart facial soft tissues were reconstructed by the Plastic Surgical team and fractures of the facial bones were managed by the Maxillofacial Surgeons.

Months later, Jim was referred to me to reconstruct his hearing and facial paralysis. The middle ear was explored and a cerebral spinal fluid leak was sealed off with a fascia graft. The disrupted middle ear bones were reconnected. A bone fragment that compressed the facial nerve was removed and the injured segment was freshened. The torn ear drum was repaired.

Two years after being pronounced dead and zipped up in a bag, Jim was very much alive. His brain deficit was minimal and his pre-injury attractive facial features were restored. The facial nerve and hearing repair efforts were successful. Jim had a slightly asymmetrical smile and adequate eyelid closure. The ear drum healed and hearing was significantly improved.

The greatest thrill for me was the greeting I received from him. Just two years after returning from the dead, he married the blond ER nurse who saved his life. They were sitting in my waiting room with a beautiful baby girl with blond curly hair. This was the most beautiful part of the fairy tale.

61)   Masked Man

I walked through the front corridor of Presbyterian Hospital on my way to visit a patient. I passed Presbyterian Hospital Level One Trauma Center and there was much commotion. The trauma team was busy with a bloody mess. I peered in to satisfy my curiosity. An unconscious patient was bleeding profusely from a gaping wound where the nose meets the forehead. The patient's face was separated from his skull. This is the most severe type of facial bone injury possible and is referred to as a LeForte III facial fracture.

Establishing an airway was critical to save his life. Attempts to intubate him failed. I stepped up. "I am a head and neck surgeon on the staff at the Eye and Ear Hospital. Would you like me to perform a tracheotomy?" There was a positive nod. I requested a trach set, put on a hospital gown, a pair of surgical gloves and performed a 20 second stab wound tracheotomy.

The Maxilla- Facial surgical team then packed the wound to control the bleeding, the more packing, the more bleeding. They pulled the jaw up to the skull and held it in place with roller gauze. This maneuver was effective. The patient was taken to the OR and I went on my way to complete my routine chores.

In the OR, the surgeons attempted to find the bleeding vessel. A torn major artery hidden deep in the wound was the most likely source of bleeding. The patient was losing more blood than could be replaced.

Once again, the wound was packed with gauze and the mandible was wired to a fixed spot on the stable skull. The wire was tightened. The bleeding stopped. This maneuver controlled the bleeding by maintaining pressure. The patient was stabilized with blood replacement. An angiographic study demonstrated a torn right internal maxillary artery.

The chief of the Maxilla-Facialsurgery service contacted me. "May, the patient was still oozing and loosing blood. We considered embolization versus trans-antral ligation. The risks with embolization are greater than compared to a trans-antral ligation. Can you reach the bleeding vessel through the trans-antral approach?" "Yes", I answered.

The chief said, "I am curious, how is it possible that you are so comfortable managing this unusual case?" I informed the chief that I arrived in Pittsburgh three weeks ago. I shared with him my previous head and neck trauma experience while serving in the "war zone".

After being invited to participate in the management of this patient, I sat down and introduced myself to the family holding vigil outside the ICU. I wanted to get the complete story and explain the critical nature of the planned procedure. I spoke to his parents and his fiancée. Communication with the patient required pencil and pad because of the tracheotomy.

The patient's name was Mike (name changed). He was an ambitious guy in his early 30s. He worked two jobs: Pittsburgh rookie police officer and part time driving a delivery truck. His near fatal accident occurred while making a delivery. He was closing the heavy doors in the back end of the truck when the hydraulic lift got stuck. Mike stuck his head in to fix the problem and just then the closing mechanism kicked in and Mike's head became wedged between the closing lift and the truck frame. He was extricated and brought to Presbyterian Hospital Trauma Center.

The family was informed that Mike was still bleeding. There was a torn vessel located behind his cheek sinus. I explained that the procedure to stop the bleeding involved an incision inside of his mouth underneath the upper lip. The front wall of the sinus is entered through a window made in the front thin bone. I indicated with my finger in my mouth the entry spot. Then I borrowed a pencil and made sketches illustrating the steps of the procedure. I told them that once in the sinus cavity, the back wall will become visible. This thin plate of bone will be cracked and removed. The end branches of the bleeding vessel should become visible (internal maxillary artery) and that I would use a binocular operating microscope to improve the visualization and individually clamp isolated branches.

"Do you have any questions?" I asked. I was prepared to provide more background, but it was clear that they were overwhelmed.

The procedure was performed that afternoon. Five vessels were identified and clipped. The next day the packing was removed and there was no bleeding. However, the euphoria of success was short lasting. That night I was called by the ICU nurse and was told that he was bleeding profusely. Once again, he was repacked to control the bleeding.

It was now 2am, Mike was bleeding around the pack and I couldn't slow it down. By this time, I had spent long hours chatting with Mike's parents and fiancée. Their wedding was postponed because of his accident. In this short period, I had won their confidence. Now there was a strong possibility that he would die, bleeding to death because I had run out of options. The night nurse working in the ICU told me to call the "Masked Man".

The nurse related, "We had a similar case last year where no one could control bleeding from an aneurysm located at the skull base. The "Masked Man" came to the rescue."
She gave me his contact number and I called. I was impressed that at 2am, he was calm and reassuring and not annoyed by my late hour call. He told me to meet him in the radiology department angiography suite in 20 minutes. I informed the anxious family members of the gravity of the situation. When I left them to take Mike to the angiography suite, they were holding hands and praying.

The angiography room was almost completely dark except for some light leaking in from the outside corridor. Mike was wheeled in on his mobile ICU bed while receiving blood from two bottles hanging from posts mounted on the bed corners. Mike looked up at me but couldn't speak because of the tracheotomy tube. He wrote on his tablet, "Am I going to make it?" I told Michael, "We are going to do our best, and the rest is up to God. "

The "Masked Man" rolled Michael into the room designated for angiography. Looking through the protective glass window, I could observe on the TV monitor and see the "Masked Man" with exquisite manual deftness direct the catheter into place and squirt some contrast into the maxillary artery. The disrupted end of the bleeding vessel was identified. Silicon pellets were injected and immediately the bleeding stopped. A miracle!

I called the family and reported that the crisis was over and Mike will be fine. I told them that I would be there in 20 minutes to explain everything. The "Masked Man" was escaping and I blocked his way. "Not so fast." I said. There was no way I could control my emotions. He was still in scrubs and wearing a surgical mask. I hugged him and kissed him on the neck. He was moved by my sincere gesture. "Please let me buy you a cup of coffee." I requested. He agreed and told me his story.

"Four years ago, I was a naval flight surgeon stationed at Lakehurst New Jersey Air Base. The military required that flight surgeons fly 10 hours per month. I was assigned to ride shot gun with a hotshot combat pilot. He flew subsonic and while making a low pass over some pines clipped the left wing. We ejected at low altitude. He burned up with the plane and I was spared death but spent two years in Walter Reed Hospital. I had more operations than I can count, mostly skin grafts.

I retooled and became an interventional radiologist. My wife left me and I live alone in an apartment near Presby. I take night calls and try to avoid being seen in public. You can see my distorted curled and scarred hands: my face looks much worse.

The navy compensated me quite well, so I have no financial worries. My real needs are satisfied whenever I can save a life. This job gives me lots of opportunities."

We finished our coffee and he disappeared into the night waiting for his next call. I never saw his face. The life saver remains the "Masked Man". What an inspiration, I thought.

At this point, it was now about 4am and exhaustion was beginning to demand that I lie down and close my eyes. I gathered my strength long enough to meet with the family. They were prepared for the worse. I described the procedure that stopped the bleeding. This was a true blessing; they were convinced that their prayers were answered.

Before I returned home, I stopped by the ICU to check on Mike. The ICU nurse was at his side taking vitals. I expressed my appreciation for finding the "Masked Man" and told her that she played a key role in saving Mike's life.

The rest of the restorative surgery was performed by members of the Maxilla-Facial and Plastic Surgery experts.

Mike married his chosen one, who incidentally was a nurse. She played a main part in his postoperative care. A year later this miracle couple returned for a follow-up except now there were three of them. They added a beautiful baby girl.

These last two stories, In the Bag and Masked Man are powerful. I learned the importance of faith; never give up hope and the supportive role of the dedicated nurse. The years of experience in the "war zone" prepared me for this moment.

62)   Bedside Save

Abe Green (name changed) was a prominent member of our congregation, Paoli Zedek (PZ). He was a holocaust survivor from Lithuania and came to Pittsburgh in 1949. He remarried and had three children. There were other relatives from Lithuania who came to Pittsburgh before the war. They all lived in Squirrel Hill, a predominantly Jewish community and all attended PZ.

Abe Green, the family patriarch, confronted me in synagogue one Sabbath morning. This was not unusual; my office travelled with me where ever I went and what better place to give an opinion than in the house of G-D. He showed me his trick. When he puffed out his cheeks or blew against pursed lips, a bulge appeared in his left neck.

"Wait!" Mr. Green said. "Listen to this." When he pushed on the mass, a definite squeaky sound was heard. The sound was like when one blows up a balloon, squeezes the end and lets the air out slowly.

"Mr. Green, I know what is wrong and your condition can be cured. Call my office and tell them I said to give you an appointment on Wednesday."

The presentation was classical and exemplified the opportunities available for me to make an accurate diagnosis based upon what can be seen even in the middle of prayer services.

The compressible mass in Mr. Green's neck was filled with air that escaped from the space between the true and false vocal cords. The definitive treatment is total excision.

On Wednesday, he came to the office for his appointment with seven members of his family. I allowed his wife and oldest son in the consultation room and the rest were requested to remain in the waiting room. I showed them a diagram illustrating his situation.

I held his hand against the front part his neck and gently pressed his fingers so he could feel the landmarks that I referred to.

"Abe, the first hard structure you feel is the hyoid and the next one down is the thyroid cartilage. The thyroid cartilage contains your vocal cords as indicated in the drawing. The small red pouch on the right is more common and is referred to as an internal laryngocele. The red structure on the left is a larger pouch that extends out into the neck between the hyoid and thyroid cartilages. That represents your situation. It is referred to as an external laryngocele. "

A CT scan confirmed my diagnosis.

The risks, options, and benefits were explained and surgery was scheduled for Monday the following week. The patient and extended family were relieved that Abe didn't have cancer. The surgery required an external incision, dissecting the balloon-like mass away from surrounding structures and following the laryngocele to its origin, the space between the true and false vocal cords. This last part was tricky. The neck of the balloon passed between the hyoid and thyroid cartilages. Access to this space required removal of a window of thyroid cartilage. The surgery was accomplished as planned and after the procedure, Abe was taken to the recovery room.

There was a 15 minute break before starting my next case. It was always pleasurable to share good news. I went up to room 517 where Mr. Green's family and friends were waiting for the doctor's update. I knew most of his family and friends from synagogue.

"The operation went well, as planned, and Abe is in the recovery room. He will be brought back to his room in about one hour. I will be back to answer your questions as soon as I finish my next scheduled surgery." Before I could retreat back to the OR, members of the family and friends wanted to shake my hand or just pat me on the back. This was their way of saying "job well done".

The second surgery was a routine procedure, ideal for allowing a resident to perform with my close supervision. After all, Eye and Ear Hospital where I worked for the first six years in Pittsburgh, was a teaching hospital. As for me, this form of teaching was the most intense. In some ways it was like a driving teacher, except the stakes are much higher. This particular resident was a senior and quite capable having performed this procedure multiple times before.

My day suddenly changed from calm to chaos. I heard over the hospital PA, "Code red, code red, room 517, room 517."

Then my peripheral vision spotted the leading members of the anesthesia department, Jay Chang and Chris Larson, racing by pushing a crash cart.

517 was Mr. Green's room! I told the resident to put the surgery on pause until I return. This was okay with the rest of the OR team. I tore off my surgical gloves and headed down the hallway past the elevator to the stairs. The OR was on the second floor. I raced up three flights two steps at a time to reach the fifth floor. Upon opening the door leading into the center hallway, I encountered a crowd of mostly Mr. Green's visitors. They blocked my progress and wanted to know what was happening. Without breaking stride, I passed them like a running-back following his blockers.

The fire door was closed between the patient wing and the entry way off the elevator. When there was a patient crisis, visitors and unessential personal were cleared from the area. I pushed open the heavy door and the corridor was clear until I reached room 517.

The excitement was palpable, like one might experience coming upon a five-alarm fire. The room was cluttered with nonessential bodies of medical students, technicians, and a Phlebotomist. The cardiac team was poised with chest paddles to shock the heart. Jay Chang was standing on a bench leaning over Mr. Green, who was yanked up over the head of his bed. Jay tried desperately to introduce a breathing tube into his trachea.

Mr. Green was unconscious and his airway was completely obstructed. His color was dusky from anoxia. My adrenalin kicked in and lessons from the war zone became reflex action. I pushed and pulled my way to the bedside. I ripped open the wound, scooped out a glob of clotted blood, used my finger instead of my eyes (Story # 7, Bailey), found the space between the vocal cords, grabbed the tube from Jay and directed it over my finger through the opened wound in the side of Mr. Green's neck. The tube was inserted through the space between the vocal cords and into the trachea. A blast of built up air, trapped below the obstruction caused by the expanding blood clot, shot out of the end of the tube. The emergency was over. Mr. Green began to breathe on his own, his color change to pink, heart rate and rhythm were strong and normal. Mr. Green was taken back to the OR where the wound was irrigated with an antibiotic-saline solution and explored for the site of bleeding. None was found and the wound was closed with a drain. Abe recovered without any sequelae and the heart, vocal cords and brain function were normal. He was discharged on Friday afternoon to be with his family for the Sabbath. Two weeks later, he was in synagogue and feeling great. Three weeks later, Abe and his wife went to Florida for their four-month winter break from Pittsburgh's cold, snow and ice. This was their routine. In January, the May family received a large carton of pink grapefruit from the Greens.

This emergency scene will never be forgotten by those who were there. My anesthesia colleagues, Jay Chang and Chris Larson, referred to this episode as "The Bedside Save".

There are times when we all play the game "what if" and this time, once again, I experienced what I felt was another miracle. I do believe one should not rely on prayer alone. We have to do our part.

63)   Brain Leak and the Insurance Executive

One day I received a call from an ENT colleague on the West Coast, "Would you be kind enough to evaluate my patient?" "Of course." I replied, intrigued. "If you agree, we will fly from San Francisco on the company private LearJet and arrive at the Allegheny County Airport located in the outskirts of Pittsburgh on the day that is convenient for you."

The appointment was set and a week later, I met Roy Jones (name changed), president of a leading health care insurance company. He was accompanied by the referral doctor. Mr. Jones was fit and tall, over six feet. His silver hair was well groomed and meticulously combed back partially covering his ears. He was dressed in leisure ware, loafers without socks, tan slacks and a patterned panama open collared shirt. He spoke with a melodic authoritative and intimidating deep tone.

However, his voice was nasal, as if he had a cold and constantly pulled out tissues to blow or wipe his dripping nose.

His history was a familiar one. Mr. Jones was miserable; he couldn't breathe through his nose. He was plagued by recurrent nasal polyps and failed to respond to long term allergy treatments, shots, avoidance food diets and lived in Phoenix Arizona for six months. It was suggested that a change in climate would eliminate inhaled pollutants as a possible cause.

My colleague, Dr. Joe Mckenna (name changed), who accompanied Mr. Jones, provided the surgical history. "Mark, Roy has been a challenge for me. Frankly, we are here out of desperation. I performed three trans-nasal endoscopic procedures in the past two years. The last operation was three months ago and the polyps are back as if he hadn't had surgery. I told Roy about your favorable experience with patients with nasal polyps. I was impressed with your presentation at the last ENT Academy Meeting in Atlanta where you reported successful management of patients with recurrent polyposis."

My ego was all pumped up. The office and OR staff were buzzing about how this V.I.P. flew in from California in his private jet to seek my care. Mr. Jones was admitted to a private suite on the top floor of Shadyside Hospital. Henry Mordoh, our hospital CEO, was alerted and Henry made a personal visit to reassure Mr. Jones, he had the best sinus surgeon and Shadyside Hospital would provide him with the best care. The night before surgery, Roy was served a lobster dinner with a bottle of expensive wine, courtesy of Mr. Mordoh.

After dinner I visited with Mr. Jones and Dr. Joe Mckenna for a pre-op meeting. We reviewed the CT scan and I pointed out that there was evidence of previous surgery. Most of the normal landmarks have been destroyed by the polyps which raised the risks of untoward side effects. I didn't reveal that the landmarks were removed by the previous surgeon. This was communicated to Joe by my glance in his direction. It was clear to me that the doctor knew that the risks were high for penetrating the orbit and creating a cerebrospinal fluid leak. I also realized that Joe Mckenna, to preserve his reputation, was wise to refer this high- profile patient out of town and far away. We were assigned the high-tech OR, the one usually used by David Zorub, the Chief of Neurosurgery. This was the largest OR equipped with the latest audiovisual technology. There was a 36 inch TV monitor mounted on three of the four OR walls. On this specific day, Chris Larson, the most competent anesthesiologist at Shadyside Hospital, took charge of giving the anesthesia. The surgery was televised for the crowd of the OR staff, my fellow, two family doctor residents on the ENT service and a University of Pittsburgh medical student. Dr. Joe McKenna was scrubbed and gowned in OR garb sitting at my side and served as my surgical assistant.

Chris Larson expertly induced light general anesthesia and supplemented this with IV narcotics. In addition to the general anesthesia, a local anesthetic was administered topically. The swollen tissues were decongested with cotton strips saturated with an epinephrine solution.

Looking into the nasal cavity of Mr. Jones with an endoscope was like looking through one's car windshield riding down a dirty winding road after a dust storm followed by a light rain. An experienced surgeon, like a sailor making his way in a fog, looks for fixed familiar landmarks for guidance.

The inferior and middle turbinates were gone. I checked for the integrity of the left lateral nasal wall that separates the eye ball from the nasal cavity by pushing on the left eye. The pressure on the eye was transmitted to inside the lateral wall of the nose. The eye on the left side was separated from the nasal cavity by only a membrane. The bony plate was gone. I would have to take extra precaution on the left side so as not to injure the eye. The lateral nasal wall on the right was intact.

Both nasal cavities were filled with leathery fibrous friable polypoid tissue; the kind of findings one encounters after previous multiple surgeries. Just a touch stirred up bleeding. There were no useful landmarks, either visible or palpable. I began to question my judgment. Did my hubris take me to a place I didn't belong?

I needed a time out to regroup. As a delaying tactic, I walked over to the x-ray view box and reviewed once more the images of Mr. Jones's paranasal sinuses. The roof of the nasal cavity, the boundary between the nose and brain appeared absent on the left side but there was no sign of dura or brain herniation. The pressure was on, all eyes were on me. I considered cancelling the surgery and admitting that the dangers of operating on a nonlife threatening condition, was too high to risk penetrating the eye or brain.

Mr. Jones had come so far and his expectations were so high, I decided to try and remove as much of the polypoid mass as possible and remain within the nasal cavity. My every move was calculated and deliberate, like trying to navigate through shallow waters with all kinds of treacherous obstacles. Striking one would have been disastrous.

I reached into the right nasal cavity, the safer side that had an intact wall between the eye, the brain and the nasal cavity. The majority of the polypoid tissue was removed. Once this was accomplished, bleeding stopped with the help of cotton strips saturated in epinephrine, a vasoconstrictor.

Those in attendance felt the tension lower. At that moment Mr. Mordoh, wearing a bunny suit, OR mask and shoe covers poked his head into the OR, "How's it going?" He was told all is well and he backed out to return to his routine.

I then had a decision to make. So far all was well. Again, thoughts raced through my mind. The evil of good is better, leave while you are ahead, and so on.

I started on the left side, the mine field side. I was careful to keep my fingers on the left eye. Any movement detected was a warning not to remove tissue grasped in my forceps but rather release and move on. The large opening between the nose and the left maxillary sinus was cleared of polyps and retained secretions in the sinus cavity were washed and cleared with suction.

Things were looking good and I was feeling better with my decision to go ahead. I stripped polypoid tissue from the roof of the anterior and posterior ethmoids. I described the entire procedure to all the observers, step by step, pointing out anatomical landmarks as encountered. Everyone present had to be impressed, especially Dr. Mckenna.

I stressed the importance to meticulously check the postoperative surgical site for bleeding and any signs of CF leakage. It was then time to address any problem encountered and take care of it.

Without a break in my narration, I spotted the sign of a CSF leak. No one else spotted it either because they were not concentrating on the fine details or they saw it but didn't realize the significance. There was a clear spot in the roof of the left posterior ethmoid. As the clear spinal fluid leaked out of the intracranial compartment, it cleared the thin film of blood over the exposed dura. It is referred to as the "Wash Out Sign".

I was not upset in any way. The patient was warned of this possibility during our post-lobster dinner conference. Dr. Mckenna was there to verify this warning. The leak was pin point in size and a perichondrial patch harvested from Mr. Jones's nasal septum worked quite well to seal the leak. The management of this unexpected sequalae was a bonus for the attendees.

Unfortunately, instead of one night to recover and fly back home, Mr. Jones was required to stay a week lying with his head slightly elevated and receive IV antibiotics. When he was fully recovered from the effects of anesthesia, I explained the situation. He was relieved to breathe through his nose and, not surprising, accepted his fate as just a temporary set- back. Dr. McKenna understood as well. He was relieved that I dealt with the CSF leak and not he. He took a commercial flight back to San Francisco and kept in touch expressing his gratefulness.

I remembered the first time that I encountered a CSF leak. It was frightening. Fortunately, I had experienced closing traumatic CSF leaks in the ear area; the management principles are similar.

This case points out a number of lessons:

1) Don't bite off more than you can chew. In other words, one must learn his limits by sound judgment rather than by learning from a disastrous outcome.

2) A surgeon is not a performer who gets paid to entertain. There was a moment when my judgment was clouded by what I perceived as crowd pressure.

3) A surgeon must leave his ego out of decision making.

4) When faced with the unexpected, deal with it.

64)   Eye and the Law Firm

I was considered an early pioneer in the field of endoscopic sinus surgery and acquired a reputation for managing the most difficult sinus conditions. This was rewarded with referrals of patients who were high risk and/or with advance disease.

Mrs. Nancy O'Brian (name changed) fit the description. She was elderly (early 70s), had chronic recurrent nasal polyps, had been operated on four times prior, was the matriarch of a distinguished family of lawyers, and her husband was the president of the Shadyside Hospital Board of Trustees and a major fund raiser. She was referred to me by the hospital CEO, Henry Mordoh.

Our first consultation set the stage for what would follow. The consultation room was filled with family members. Her stately husband stood by his wife's side. He wore a double-breasted tweed wool suit, a gold time piece with chain that was tucked into his waist pocket. I noticed his prominent gold mason's ring on his right middle finger. Two of Mrs. O'Brian's sons were present as well. I learned that there were five sons and all of them worked in the family firm, who's name listed the name O'Brian six times to represent each one. Personally, I thought it would have been easier to display the name of their firm on the door or stationary if they chose, O'Brian & Sons. One of them made sure to let me know that their firm was best known for medical malpractice.

Nancy O'Brian was suffering from her condition. Out of embarrassment, she covered her nose with a fine laced handkerchief to cover the polyps that protruded from her nostrils. Her lips were dry and crusted which was a telltale sign that she was an obligatory mouth breather. A review of a recent CT scan revealed that her nasal cavity and each of the sinus complexes were opaque. None of the usual landmarks were present, this picture was caused by diffuse polyposis and retained secretions in spite of multiple previous sinus operations.

Mrs. O'Brian was a petite lady, five feet tall and maybe 110 pounds. She was sweet with a twinkle in her eyes. Her appearance was disarming. In spite of her presentation, it became clear that she was the boss. A number of times she told her family members that she was perfectly capable to answer the doctor's questions and to "shush".

I made drawings, showed diagrams and answered all questions to be sure that everyone present was clear as to the risks and possible sequalae. I wrote down a list that included bleeding, blood transfusion, leakage of brain fluid, brain penetration, eye injury and blindness and added that death was a remote possibility.

Frankly, I was praying that they would reject the surgical option. The family got the message and urged Mrs. O'Brian to think about it before scheduling. One son made it clear that he was strongly against surgery. Mrs. O'Brian interrupted the discussion, "Please schedule as soon as possible. I can't live with this condition. I accept the risks."

The surgery was difficult because the conditions were similar to the case of the insurance executive, no landmarks and control of bleeding became an issue. Blood transfusion was rarely required for sinus surgery and blood replacement was not prepared for her.

My mission was to restore her nasal airway. This entailed the removal of the gross collection of polypoid tissue, enlarging the opening between the nasal cavity and maxillary sinuses, and irrigating out retained secretions. The bleeding continued until the nasal cavity was packed. Once the bleeding was controlled, the patient was allowed to awaken from general anesthesia. I discovered that the patient was hypertensive during the procedure and this explained the unusual amount of bleeding. Upon emerging from anesthesia, her blood pressure elevated to a dangerous level. Her systolic pressure recorded 280 and diastolic was 210. Her blood pressure recorded pre-operatively was normal; 120 over 80.

My "go to" anesthesiologist was called in. When Chris Larson arrived on the scene, I felt things would Improve. Chris, using appropriate medications, lowered the blood pressure to a safe range. She was extubated and taken to the OR recovery room. I took off my bloody gloves and stripped down to my green OR garb to meet with the anxious family of malpractice lawyers.

As suspected, O'Brian and sons were out in full strength in the waiting room. "Your Mom is doing fine; she is in the recovery room." I reported to them. Just then, over the hospital PA system, "Dr. May to the recovery room, STAT!"

Mrs. O'Brian was bleeding through her nasal pack. The nurse reported that the patient had become agitated, sat up and had to be restrained. Her blood pressure shot up and then the bleeding started. I noticed that her left eye was ecchymotic; the eye lids were swollen shut. Upon pulling the lids apart, I noted that the eye was prominent, fixed, and the pupil dilated. The eye felt tense when I gently pushed on it.

These new findings suggested an intraorbital hemorrhage and required immediate attention. There was a small window of one hour to correct the problem or risk losing vision. My first thought was to obtain an eye consult. At Shadyside Hospital, unlike Presbyterian Hospital, there were no eye residents and I requested calling the private doctor on call. No one responded. I remembered my days at HGP and ordered an ophthalmometer and tonometer. One instrument was to measure the amount of outward displacement and the other was to measure intraocular pressure. The left eye was 4mm more prominent than the normal right eye. The tonometer measurement was most troubling; the pressure was 60 compared to 15, the upper limits of normal.

The team was notified and we were back in the OR. Mrs. O'Brian was intubated and once again under general anesthesia. Before going to the OR, I stopped by the waiting room and informed the family of the new development.

My goal was to find the source of bleeding and decompress the eye. As long as the eye was under pressure, the blood supply to the optic nerve was compromised. This is what leads to blindness. There were two possible sites of bleeding, the anterior ethmoid and/or the sphenopalatine artery. Based upon the site of surgery, the anterior ethmoid was the most likely source of bleeding. When I removed the nasal packing to inspect the surgical site, the tense left eye and its prominence were immediately reduced. I had to replace the pack because otherwise there was a risk that she would die from blood loss. My task was clear; save her life and her vision. The bleeding was controlled with the pack, thus prioritizing decompressing the eye.

I recalled my previous experience with orbital decompression for exophthalmos associated with hyperthyroidism learned while working with Dr. Ogura. The surgery involved working inside the maxillary sinus through a Caldwell Luc approach. The first step was to remove the party wall between the orbit and the nasal cavity. In this case it was already removed by previous sinus surgery. The next step required removal of the roof of the sinus (the floor of the orbit). It was removed and orbital fat was teased into the maxillary sinus cavity. The eye tension and pressure were immediately relieved and returned to near normal levels.

The sphenopalatine vessel was isolated in the pterygopalatine fossa accessed through a window created in the posterior wall of the maxillary sinus. This vessel was micro-clipped. Next, the anterior ethmoid artery was isolated as it coursed though it's tiny ostia from the nasal side to the orbit. It was clamped closed with a micro-clip.

The pack was removed and there was no bleeding. Once again, she was extubated and returned to the recovery room. It was now 10pm; the ordeal started at 2pm when Mrs. O'Brian was taken to the OR.

I related all that transpired to the family. They were worn out and emotionally spent. This explained their lack of questions.

"Doctor, you must be exhausted. Go home and get some rest." Mr. O'Brian said to me.

I returned at 6am, as was my routine, to check all my patients before starting another day of surgery. Mrs. O'Brian was sitting on the edge of her bed.

"Doctor, what happened?" Her voice was hoarse and her breathing was definitely labored and stridorous. I inspected her vocal cords and there was a web of shredded mucosa that formed a web occluding 90 percent of the space between her vocal cords. This most likely was due to repeated and prolonged intubation. "War zone" training demanded that when one thinks about it, one goes for it! This was referring to creating an emergency airway by performing a tracheotomy.

I placed Mrs. O'Brian in a wheel chair and briskly took her to the OR. The personnel were preparing the ORs for that day's schedule. I spotted the head nurse of the OR, "I have an emergency: I need a trach set and another pair of hands for an assist."

Mrs. O'Brian could not breathe lying down, so a sitting up trach was done under local anesthesia.

Upon completion of the trach, her breathing quickly changed from labored to normal. When we returned to her room from the OR there were a bunch of O'Brian family members waiting. After a night's sleep, the attorneys were prepared with their extra-long yellow paper legal- tablets filled with questions. The mother anticipated what was coming. She took hold of a tablet and printed in big letters. "BACK OFF, HE SAVED MY LIFE!"

Her labs showed a reduced H & H (Hemoglobin & Hematocrit) indicating she had lost 25 percent of her blood volume. Joel Weinberg, the medical consultant, ordered two units of blood. The sons stepped up, "We will donate the blood." I explained that there was not enough time and that she needed it ASAP. She was discharged after ten days of hell, one life threatening crisis after another. I began to get bad vibes and a lawsuit seemed eminent. The first indication was a court order to turn in all records related to the O'Brian case. Another came from my lawyer friend, Stanley Greenfield. He asked me about the case and tried to cheer me up.

"They love you! It is the anesthesiologist, Chris Larson, which they are after. "He explained to me. After reviewing the records, they faulted him for not controlling the blood pressure. I found this infuriating, considering it was Chris who controlled the blood pressure. Besides, no one was at fault. This was a perfect example of what appeared to be routine, and unexpected serious issues were met with appropriate heroic measures.

I requested that the patient return every week on Sunday mornings at 7am before they went to church. I explained that this was a quiet time, no traffic, and plenty of parking. I didn't tell them about my policy dealing with PO complications or disgruntled patients. It's a big mistake to have someone in that category mixed in with the general population sitting in a busy waiting room.

The outcome was spectacular. Her eye doctor reported that a new eye glass lens corrected the postoperative double vision, otherwise visual acuity returned to the pre-op state. Her nasal airway remained functional and the surgical wounds from the trach and the other incisions healed with scars that were barely noticeable.

After several months of chit chat and tender love and care with Mrs. O'Brian and her boys, I was able to earn their love, respect and confidence. The lawsuit was dropped.

Chapter 8

Medical Malpractice

65)   Law, Lawyers, Judges and Juries

Credit "Complications" by Atul Gawande published 2002.

Gawande on page 57 of his Award Winning book, Complications, refers to research of Troyen Brennan, a Harvard professor of law and public health who failed to find evidence that litigation reduces medical error rates. The likelihood of winning a malpractice lawsuit depended more on outcome than extent of disease or unavoidable risks of care. Furthermore, the tort system makes adversaries of patient and physician. I discovered that the work of Professor Brennen, as reported by Gawande, coincided with my personal experience with the medical malpractice system as one who has been sued and as an expert witness.

Once I was established as a recognized expert in managing facial nerve and sinus disorders, plaintiff and defense medical malpractice attorneys sought my opinion. During the last ten years of private practice, I agreed to testify on an average of twice a year. I represented both defendants and plaintiffs depending on the merits of the case. My willingness to participate in the system was greatly influenced by my close friend Stanley Greenfield, a well- known Pittsburgh litigator. Accepting this role as an expert witness was appealing to my sense of fairness and an opportunity to pursue the truth. It turned out, based on my limited and anecdotal experience, that the system in specific instances did not seem fair or truthful. In spite of my objections and perceived flaws in the legal process, a patient has the right to be compensated for damages as a result of substandard care. In all cases, there is a painful reality for the physician who receives a complaint; the implication is guilty as charged until proven otherwise.

My story about the Medico- Legal system began in 1974, just one month after leaving 14 years of academic life, 14 years without ever having been sued. I was called to a large Pittsburgh Hospital facility, one that was not part of the University system and one without a trauma center. The doctor on the phone, I found out later, was a physiatrist who had limited surgical experience; he was the designated on call doc for the ER that night.

The chronology of the story I am about to relate was remarkable and the outcome inevitable.

An unmarried young man in his early 20s, a carpenter by profession, was returning from a job. He was driving in a heavy downpour on a wet, winding, and narrow two lane back country Pennsylvania road on his way to his mom's house for a family dinner. He lost control, skidded into a tree, and was thrown through the windshield. This occurred at around 6pm on a weekday evening in front the PA State Trooper's head-quarters in Latrobe Pennsylvania.

The trauma victim was immediately transported to the closest available hospital. The patient arrived at this rural hospital where first aid was administered. A pressure dressing was applied to the puncture wound in his left mid-lateral neck. Aside from spitting up fresh blood, the visible external bleeding appeared to be minimal. Blood was drawn and sent to the lab for routine tests. Vital signs were recorded, and radiographs were taken of his chest, cervical spine and skull. An un-displaced C-6 cervical spine fracture was the only positive finding.

On initial examination, the patient seemed stable with normal vitals and a blood count in the normal range. Now at 7pm, an hour after the accident, the ER nurse expressed her concerns. The vital signs had changed dramatically. The blood pressure dropped from normal noted on admission, to 90 over 60 and the pulse was rapid and weak. His skin was pale and clammy. This young man was hemorrhaging and needed blood replacement. After cross match and type, blood transfusion was started.

The on-call surgeon assigned to cover the ER that night was consulted. She was an abdominal surgeon and she did not feel competent to manage head and neck wounds. She suspected that the patient was swallowing massive amounts of blood and recommended immediate transfer to a larger facility located in Pittsburgh proper where a head and neck surgeon would be available.

It was 8pm, two hours after the accident when the young man with the puncture wound arrived at hospital number two. The physiatrist was helpless and incapable to do much more than to continue blood replacement started at the first hospital. He desperately called two surgeons and three ENT specialists. They were either not available or declined to respond on the grounds that the problem was not in their area of expertise. My call came at 9pm. I arrived fifteen minutes later. The patient was conscious and coherent. He held a plastic suction tip in his mouth to handle the bleeding coming up from his pharynx. He insisted that he be allowed to sit up; he was drowning in his own blood. The faster blood was replaced, the greater the hemorrhage.

I knew immediately the site of bleeding and the remedy. This case was familiar to me; a flash back to the "war zone". I recalled a lady brought to HGP ER (story #47) with massive bleeding from her mouth. She had been stabbed in the neck, the same place where the young carpenter's neck was penetrated by a glass chard from his car windshield.

In the HGP case, the knife lacerated the jugular vein glanced off the thyroid cartilage and sliced a hole in her pharynx. The jugular vein a high volume, low pressure conduit emptied into her pharynx and presented as massive bleeding from her mouth. Much of the blood loss went undetected as she swallowed most of it. The case of the carpenter looked like a replica of the lady with the knife wound.

Immediate action was required to save this young man's life. Just as with the knife wound victim, an emergency tracheotomy, a packing stuffed into her mouth and pharynx to stop the bleeding, neck exploration and ligation of the jugular vein saved her life. That was at HGP where there was a team poised and ready to put out a fire without concern for legal consequences.

I found myself in a dilemma; perform heroic surgery with only the doctor who did not know the difference between a surgical clamp and a shoe horn, or transport the patient to the University's level one trauma center and run the risk that the patient might bleed out in the transport ambulance.

The ambulance arrived at Presby's ER moments before I did. I left my car parked at the front entrance and dashed into

Presby's ER with the security guard chasing after me; I wasn't wearing my ID badge. He backed off when I entered the ER and he saw me go into action. The patient was unconscious and his skin was blanched; his pulse and blood pressure were barely perceptible. He was receiving his 5th and 6th bottles of blood. Jay Chang was one of the best anesthesiologists that I had ever met. He responded to my call that the patient was on his way and was waiting for the patient when brought in by the ambulance crew.

It was now 10pm. Jay was able to intubate the patient in spite of a cervical spine fracture and a pharynx filled with blood. As soon as the tube passed into the trachea, frothy foam rose up in the endotracheal tube, a sign of pulmonary edema due to heart failure. This was followed by cardiac arrest and a flat EKG in spite of every effort to save his life.

My nightmare became a reality: as the last treating physician, I had to inform the family that their son, brother, and friend died. They never heard me say, "We did everything we could".
I cleaned up and headed home. This was a first for me and I was emotionally drained. At a time like this, one's mind goes into super drive. How could a young healthy not yet 30 year- old with his entire life before him walk into a hospital after surviving a car wreck with only a small neck wound and 4 hours later be dead.

The dead carpenter's grieving and angry family contacted the new lawyer in town. The lawyer was less than six months out of law school, just passed his boards, and hadn't tried a single case. Based on a review of the hospital records and some depositions he successfully sued three hospitals and nine doctors including me, guilty by association. I was advised by my medical malpractice defense lawyer, "Don't fight it! Settle the case, let our lawyers negotiate settlement."

I was counseled by my insurance carrier that the story was so incriminating and the outcome so disastrous, if heard by a jury, I could be found liable for a sum beyond my coverage of a million dollars. The other real threat was trial by the newspapers. One can only imagine the headlines, the embarrassment, and the suggestion that I was a bad doctor.

Then it occurred to me; who testified that I didn't meet the standard of care? An expert witness would have to make this claim. What basis would they have? I did everything right. Did the process take into consideration my years of unique experience in the "war zone"?

I discovered that the lawsuit against me was based on the testimony of the Chairman of Surgery of the University of Pittsburgh. He didn't know me. He never bothered to study the details of this case or inquire as to my background or level of competence. What could have been his motive? Was his testimony based on the fee he received from the lawyer? I doubted that. More than likely it was politically based. This was a case for General Surgery and not ENT. The Chairman of Surgery was protecting his turf. So often experts forget that decisions for or against a defendant or plaintiff should be fact based and not for personal gain. It should not be based on money, ego, politics or any other hidden agenda.

66)   Operated on the Wrong Side

1986 was my year for lawsuits. I hadn't been sued for over 12 years and then I got hit by a cluster of five in a row. Three were nuisance cases, one might have led to my murder, and the last had merit.

The three nuisance cases were eventually dropped due to lack of merit. In the meantime I was forced to take time to review records, answer questions in written form and at depositions.

Upon receiving a complaint, my malpractice insurance company advised me not to communicate with the patient. From this moment on, contact would be limited to attorneys, representing plaintiff, and the insurance carrier. This practice destroyed the patient/physician relationship and created an adversarial climate.

The insurance company provided me with an attorney and payout coverage up to $500,000. The state of Pennsylvania provided an additional $500,000 as part of a catastrophe fund (Cat Fund) in the event that the plaintiff was successful.

The first nuisance case involved Carol (name changed), a 32 year old attractive young woman who was obsessed with a bump on the bridge of her nose. The risks, options, and benefits were explained to her. Pictures were taken to document the preoperative deformity. Her postoperative result was so pleasing that her older sister, who had a similar deformity, made an appointment to be evaluated and was scheduled for rhinoplasty.

All was well until three months after Carol's surgery. Her new obsession was an irregularity that was detected by touch only. There was a palpable irregularity along the left lateral side of her nasal bone where the chisel cut was created for the osteotomy. This cut was made along the naso-facial line on both sides and allowed the surgeon to infracture the nasal bones to narrow the nasal pyramid. The infracture also closed the open roof created by the bump removal. This was an acceptable occurrence after rhinoplasty and would become less noticeable with time.

Carol was impatient and was convinced that her doctor did something wrong. She found a lawyer that promised to get her money at no charge to her. He took me through the process hoping my insurance company would write him a check for at least $50,000.

Based on the spectacular improvement comparing the pre and post- op photos, the plaintiff's attorney advised the patient to withdraw her complaint.

The outcome was the same in the two other nuisance cases.

Patients likely to sue have been profiled; they are demanding, have unrealistic expectations, request guarantees, are overly complimentary, and have previously sued a doctor. The five patients who sued me in 1986 did not seem to fit any profile.

In most cases, the patient was interested in winning the jack pot without any skin in the game because there are lawyers who encourage malpractice lawsuits by taking the cases on a contingency basis. Doctors have been sued by patients who claim they love their doctor and the lawsuit is not personal but strictly business. After all Doctor, they would claim, it is not *your* money, it is the insurance company's money and they have plenty of it.

The patient who wanted to murder me gave plenty of warning and I should have seen it coming. Roger (name changed) was a sad sack, a "Mr. Joe Btfspik", the character from the Little Abner

Sunday newspaper comic strip. This is the man who walks under a dark cloud; gets splashed by a car that drives through the only puddle on the block just as he walks by, gets in the wrong line at the bank and so on.

Nothing goes right in Roger's life; his dog ran away, his wife was totally dependent, and he never had anything in his life that worked properly. He had a prostate procedure and had impotence and incontinence ever since forcing him to wear a diaper. He had routine abdominal surgery for gall bladder disease and had a complication that required him to wear a colostomy bag.

He came to me with a deep parotid mass. He was previously operated two years earlier. A total parotidectomy was performed to remove a mixed tumor involving the deep lobe. An MRI report indicated that this mass was most likely recurrent and was located deep in his neck between his mouth and jaw. A fluoroscopic directed needle biopsy was not diagnostic; a malignancy could not be excluded.

After a long discussion of the risks, options and benefits, I explained that doing nothing would allow this tumor to continue to enlarge. It was possible to remove it now but as it grows larger with time that option may not be available. He elected to schedule surgery.

I explained that the major risk was damage to the facial nerve. I showed him what happened when the facial nerve was damaged. I pulled my facial skin down with my hand producing an eye that doesn't close and a mouth that sags. I intentionally had our conversation witnessed by my nurse and a member of his family. I insisted that the conversation was documented and signed.

Roger said the words of warning, "I trust you doctor, you are highly recommended". When I heard these compliments, I should have referred the patient to another doctor. This was the type of patient that should be referred out, given three names and to be certain that none of my friends were on the list.

The tumor was removed. Unfortunately, the nerve was imbedded in scar tissue from the previous surgery and was injured; the divided nerve ends were repaired with sutures. After surgery, Roger was depressed and despondent. Before the facial surgery, he had a hound dog sagging face and resembled Walter Mathau. Now the sagging was more pronounced. The right eye was wide open and red from exposure and there was drooling from the right corner of his mouth. Roger told me he was miserable and there was no reason to go on with his life. He looked like a freak. He lost his one pleasure since it was impossible for him to read.

As was my policy with disgruntled patients, I met with Roger each week an hour before starting regular office hours. It became apparent that Roger needed professional help. I became concerned that his suicidal ideology would be actuated. I contacted his son and shared my concerns. After six months, there was evidence of some recovery but not enough to overcome the extreme facial sagging. The family warned me that their dad purchased a hand gun. I arranged to never be alone with him, especially when Roger told me how much he hated me and wanted to kill me. A week later, a letter from his lawyer arrived. This lawsuit was provoked by hate and desire for revenge.

The plaintiff could not find an expert witness to testify that the injury was caused by a departure from the standard of care. The lawsuit was dropped.

Roger died from a heart condition before the lawsuit materialized.

My last medical malpractice lawsuit was meritorious because I operated on the wrong side. How could that happen? Even I would be hypercritical of such a happening. Yet it has happened to the most experienced, cautious, conscientious, and principled surgeons. I surveyed my colleagues and found that operating on the wrong side is not as uncommon as one would think.

In my case, the patient, Harriet (name changed) was a single lady in her late 50s who worked as a secretary for a prestigious law firm. She complained of a weak gravelly voice that followed a URI. The problem had persisted for over a year. She had a paralyzed vocal cord secondary to a viral infection since no cause could be found. Her voice was recorded and the vocal cords were visualized, videotaped with and without stroboscopic lighting.

I referred Harriet to a respected University based voice therapist. No improvement was achieved after six months of treatment. I discussed re-innervating her paralyzed left vocal cord using the Tucker procedure (story #45). At that time, I had successfully restored or improved the voice in ten patients using this technique. After viewing the documentation in several patients, she agreed to schedule surgery.

The surgery was performed two weeks before our planned family ski vacation. She returned three weeks PO and was seen by a colleague who covered my practice. He called to report Harriet wanted to know why her neck surgical scar was on the right when the surgery was for her paralyzed left vocal cord. I instructed him to arrange for her to see me in one week when I returned.

There was no defense; I operated on the wrong side in spite of every effort to prevent this. I tried to win back her confidence by pointing out that her voice is stronger although the voice quality hasn't improved. I viewed her vocal cords with a flexible scope and camera so we could look at her vocal cords together. I recorded the findings and reviewed them with her comparing the preoperative situation with the post-op findings. In my opinion, no damage occurred. The normal cord was fuller than before and extended across the mid-line providing better contact with the paralyzed atrophic left vocal cord. This created a stronger voice than before the surgery. From her body language it was clear I wasn't making the sale.

She didn't return for her three month follow-up visit. The Shadyside Hospital record room secretary notified me that a copy of Harriet's records have been requested by the law firm of Brown & Brown (name changed). Brown & Brown was a small firm consisting of a husband and wife practicing law together. These two had themselves a "slam dunk" case with deep pockets. I'd had dealings with them previously and they were upset with me when I decided not to testify for them against a Pittsburgh colleague.

One week after copies of Harriet's records were sent to Brown & Brown, two men in uniform visited my office. One was the sheriff and the other was his deputy. They were wearing spotless freshly pressed brown sheriff's uniforms. A shiny five pointed star was pinned to their shirts. They wore cowboy hats, and pearl handled guns were visible in their holsters. The two of them stormed into my crowded waiting room and announced in a loud booming voice, "We are here for Doctor May." They were sent by Brown & Brown to serve me a summons to appear in their office for a discovery deposition.

This was the beginning of Brown & Brown's intimidation program. Without going into detail, this outrageous behavior continued until the day of trial. Brown & Brown threatened me with going after my personal assets beyond the million dollar insurance coverage. They argued that operating on the wrong side was an egregious departure from the standard of care and represented gross negligence beyond acceptability. They threatened me with criminal charges.

"All rise for the honorable Judge Bryan" (name changed), called out the court officer. It was now 10am and the trial began. The jury of my peers were chosen and in place. Facing me was an assortment of characters. They didn't look friendly to me. Before opening statements Judge Bryan called the lawyers to the front. They conferred and departed the courtroom into the judge's chambers.

An hour later, the court officer announced the case was settled and the jury was dismissed. Later that day I received a call from my attorney. Mrs. Brown's parent had died just as the trial began. My insurance company appointed attorney made an offer to settle without trial. They arrived at 500,000 dollars and both parties agreed.

A week passed. I got a call from my medical malpractice representative; the company was dropping me as a client.

"What does that mean?" The agent said, "It means that you have no coverage. The computer spit you out as a bad risk."

I called Chicago, the main office of my insurance carrier. I inquired and learned the name of the CEO and requested that I speak with him. To my surprise he took my call. "Mr. Smyth (name changed), this is Professor Doctor Mark May from the University of Pittsburgh. I have testified for your company as an expert witness on a number of occasions, undoubtedly saving the company millions of dollars. I have been informed by your Pittsburgh agent that the company has cancelled my coverage." "Let me call you back." He said. Ten minutes later ... "No problem, you are covered, sorry for that."

I was accused by Brown & Brown of being reckless and careless and being more interested in making money than the welfare of the patient. They accused me of being too busy making money than to pay attention to detail for the sake of my patient. This characterization may impress a jury to award the highest cash settlement but is far from the truth.

Operating on the wrong side can occur when every precaution is taken; drawings of the lesion labeled right and left, radiographs displayed on a view box in the OR, and nurses and anesthesia personnel all checking.

Injected the Wrong Side

I was injected on the wrong side of my face while fully alert and didn't realize it until after the injection. The doctor was a full professor and chairman of a department. In this instance, Botox was injected for facial spasm. The normal side of my face was weakened for six weeks. My response was measured and understanding. He made a mistake proving that it is human to error, doctors are not robots. Personally, I would rather trust a human than a robot. Try talking to a robot.

Facial Nerve and Parotid Surgery

A department chairman at a major university in California was sued for cutting a facial nerve in a patient with a small benign tumor. Plaintiff lawyers refer to a case like this as a "slam dunk." The case went to court against the advice of the malpractice insurance carrier. The professor convinced the jury that no one is perfect. He had performed over a 100 of these procedures without injuring the facial nerve. On this occasion, the anatomy was different. The anatomy is different in every patient. In spite of his best efforts, the nerve was cut. Injuries to the facial nerve occur one in one hundred cases. This was the one in 100. The jury decided in his favor and the case was dismissed.

Blind Eye and Sinus Surgery

An ENT colleague, who practiced in Lake Havasu, Arizona, was sued for penetrating his patient's eye during sinus surgery. This resulted in blindness. My friend successfully defended himself at trial. He had the jury mesmerized as they leaned forward to view the video taken at the time of the surgery. He described the close relationship between the eye and the diseased sinus. The jury listened to his every word and realized the technical difficulty and proximity of the eye to the diseased sinuses.

Personal Comments:
I will demonstrate that the judge, lawyers and witnesses for defendant and plaintiff play a key role.

The cases described are exceptions. To my knowledge, it is rare to be able to successfully defend blindness following sinus surgery or accidentally cutting the facial nerve during routine parotid surgery unless there are extenuating circumstances.

In my opinion, these two cases demonstrated the importance of the effectiveness of the defendant's testimony, the venue and the jury.

Not a single doctor is immune; not the ones just starting out, nor the most experienced ones. There are some specialties that seem more vulnerable and others less likely to be sued. If a baby is born with any kind of deformity, it is assumed that the doctor committed malpractice. The opposite is the experience of head and neck cancer specialists.

A baby was born with a paralyzed face. The delivery was by forceps. There is a legal term Res Ipsa Loquitur, the fact speaks for itself. The jury assumes that all babies are born normal and if not, the doctor must have done something wrong. I defended the doctor because the newborn had the classic signs of other congenital defects, like a deformed kidney and absence of the external ear on the paralyzed side. The jury paid no attention to my testimony. They looked at the deformed baby and awarded the family more than a million dollars.

A famous mid-western specialist in cancer of the head and neck operated on a patient with cancer of the vocal cords. The cancer was primarily on the right vocal cord extending to the left side. The surgical approach to save speaking and swallowing and remove the cancer required that the surgeon remove all of the right side and part of the left side of the voice mechanism. This famous surgeon mistakenly removed all of the left side and had to perform a total laryngectomy leaving a permanent breathing hole in the patient's neck.

There was no lawsuit; the patient was grateful that the surgeon cured the cancer.

67)   Expert Witness

The stories included in this section represent highlights of my experience as an expert medical witness. The cases involved managing the facial nerve and sinus disorders. Usually, the process started with a personal call from an attorney. "Would you be willing to review a case for us?" My decision to take or turndown a case was dependent on merit of the case.

Dental Numbness & Lack of Informed Consent

I represented two different doctors who both had identical claims charged against them. One was tried in the Washington County Court in Washington, PA and the other in a Washington District Court in Washington, DC.

Each plaintiff claimed that following an endo-nasal sinus surgical procedure, they suffered from permanent disabling numbness of their upper teeth on one side. The main difference in these two cases was the venue and plaintiff lawyer. The defense lawyer was the same in both cases because both doctors had the same malpractice insurance carrier. The lawyer won in favor of the defendant doctor in Washington, PA so it was natural for the same lawyer to be appointed to defend the second doctor.

At the time of each trial, I showed drawings of the fibers that passed by the surgical site on their way to the upper teeth. I stressed that although dental numbness had been reported, this rarely occurred.

The Washington, DC lawyer won his case for the plaintiff based upon the lack of informed consent; the surgeon failed to warn the patient of possible dental numbness even though it rarely occurs. This is a question for every surgeon, must they warn a patient of every possible complication? The favorable verdict for the patient was based solely on lack of informed consent. The plaintiff was awarded $175,000.

Eye Injury

A plaintiff sued a doctor because of permanent double vision after sinus surgery. The surgeon reported eye penetration during removal of polyps from the ethmoid sinus. I argued for the defendant that upon reviewing the preoperative CT scans, the polyps eroded the party wall between the eye and ethmoid sinus. Further, the anatomical proximity raised the risk factor of eye encroachment.

The jury found in our favor. I returned home feeling good until a call came from the defense lawyer. He explained that the plaintiff's attorney appealed the case and brought in a University Radiologist, a specialist who read sinus CT scans. He refuted my testimony and claimed that an ENT surgeon was not qualified to read radiographs. That wasn't even the contested issue. It was whether the risk of eye injury was explained as a possibility and was part of the informed consent. In this case there was a $350,000 payout. Again, the plaintiff never established lack of informed consent or departure of standard of care. The jury's decision was based on the magnitude of the injury.

Sushi Man

Ten years after I retired, a plaintiff lawyer from Seattle met me in a Denver Colorado sushi restaurant. He wanted to know if his case had any merit. His client developed Bell's Palsy 10 days after a car crash. I provided testimony to support his client's claim. Barry Schaitkin, my friend and colleague, was hired by the liability insurance carrier. Barry was a recognized facial nerve expert; he worked with me for five years and coauthored our classic book, <u>The Facial Nerve</u>. I quoted a statement from our book that supported delayed facial palsy following trauma. Presumably, this is caused by delayed post-traumatic facial nerve swelling. My testimony persuaded the jury to find in favor of the Sushi Man's client.

Grimacing Post Dental Injection

A lawyer for a medical malpractice insurance carrier asked me to review a most fascinating case. The records were voluminous; three boxes including three professionally made 20 minute video documentations. The Chicago-Medical Malpractice law firm represented the plaintiff and was ready to try their case. However, there was one piece missing; the testimony of the defense expert witness. I was scheduled for a discovery deposition to be conducted in my office in Pittsburgh.

I was warned that the lead attorney for this firm never lost a case. Forewarned, I spent twenty hours preparing. The plaintiff sued her dentist. She claimed after her dentist performed a traumatic mandibular nerve block, she was incapacitated with an uncontrollable facial grimacing that has destroyed her social life and her career as a semi- professional actress. She sang and danced in summer theater shows. She claimed to be popular at church productions and local entertainment clubs.

The most appealing evidence that supported her claim was the professionally edited and produced movies that demonstrated her facial condition pre and post dental injection.

One of the video documentations submitted for my review demonstrated her facial grimacing that plagued her and was attributed to the dental injection. She displayed a grotesque array of facial distortions. This gross facial disfigurement would undoubtedly impress a jury. The insurance company was ready to negotiate a settlement without a jury trial.

The patient claimed that when the dentist pushed the needle into her jaw, she felt a bolt of lightning and when she got home her face felt numb. Two days later, the facial grimacing began. This description was typical of an injection close to or into the mandibular nerve and not the facial nerve. I noted upon review of her submitted video tapes that the grimacing didn't fit any known pathologic pattern. In my opinion, the grimacing was either conversion hysteria or malingering for psychological or financial gain.

I shared these observations with the insurance company lawyer. She informed me that this kind of accusation was difficult to prove and required hiring a psychiatrist. Our psychiatrist would argue with the opposing psychiatrist; we ran the risk that the jury might turn against us. Besides, we were not budgeted to hire a psychiatrist.

I countered that our strongest position was to demonstrate that it was impossible to reach the facial nerve with a dental needle used to perform a mandibular block as in this case. It would strengthen our case if we had drawings made by a medical artist and to acquire an Oro-maxillo-facial surgeon to serve as our expert witness. Again, the insurance attorney reminded me that it was too close to trial. It was difficult to enter new evidence at this late date. Besides, there were no funds to hire another expert or have drawings made.

The insurance company hired a private detective who secretly video-taped the budding actress first thing in the morning while she walked her dog and greeted neighbors. Videos were taken with a camera and a telephoto-lens mounted inside a delivery truck parked outside of her house. This ploy failed to detect any facial abnormality. Based on these findings and my observations, the insurance company reconsidered and decided to go to trial.

Chicago was cold and windy that morning as I walked to the courthouse. The courtroom was ready, opposing attorneys in place, and the jury anxious to hear this case. The plaintiff attorney was impressive as he laid out his case. One got the feeling that the jury sympathized with the plight of the actress.

The Chicago plaintiff lawyer who never lost a case, successfully argued pretrial before the judge to disallow the candid videos taken by our private detective and to avoid any reference to my diagnosis of hysteria, conversion hysteria and malingering for financial gain.

The verdict for or against depended on whether the Chicago lawyer could get me to state that it was possible for the dental needle to reach the facial nerve. I insisted in my pretrial deposition and so far after repeatedly being asked and answered, that it was not possible to reach the facial nerve with the dental needle designed for a mandibular block.

He countered, "That is your opinion. How do you account for our experts, a medical school Professor of Anatomy, a University Radiologist, a University Professor of Dental Surgery, and the Chairman of a University Anesthesiology Department who all disagree with you?"

I answered, "The difference is that the facial nerve is my specialty. I have been studying the facial nerve for 30 years, which is why my opinion is valid."

"Doctor May, may I ask you some questions regarding the facial nerve?" I nodded.

"Your honor, please advise the witness to indicate verbally so the members of the jury can hear his response."

The Chicago lawyer intended to treat me as a hostile witness. He began with a list of questions that were likely prepared for him by an ENT board examiner. He was attempting to disqualify me as an expert witness. It didn't take me long to realize that the questions were taken from my book, The Facial Nerve. With each question, I not only answered correctly, I provided the chapter and the page number as well.

"Ok Doctor, let us look at this human skull. Is this the skull that you used for your earlier testimony?"
"Yes."
"Do you recall demonstrating with the dental needle that on this skull the needle couldn't reach the facial nerve?"
"Yes, that is correct."
"Do you recall testifying that no two skulls are identical and that is how one can distinguish a plastic molded artificial skull from a real skull?"
"Yes."
"Doctor May, is it possible that there could be a skull where the needle could reach the facial nerve?"
"Yes."

I thought this answer was true. For example, one could find a skull of a midget, a child, or a small person where the needle would reach the facial nerve. I controlled myself and didn't add this caveat to avoid sounding cute. It was these kinds of statements that can turn a jury against the one testifying. Pretrial, I was counseled by the insurance attorney to give honest answers, keep them short, not to be argumentative and not to attempt to be a lawyer. She assured me that I would be given an opportunity to explain my position.

I was shocked and let down when the judge asked the insurance attorney, "Do you have any questions for Doctor May?"
"No further questions, your honor."

The insurance company attorney declined the opportunity to clarify my answer. Was it possible that she committed legal malpractice? That possibility haunted me until after the case was settled between the opposing attorneys for $750,000. She was instructed by the insurance company representative to settle before the jury verdict. The insurance carrier feared a multi-million dollar verdict.

This was the second case that I lost and the largest settlement awarded against a client that I represented. In my opinion, the outcome in this case was David versus Goliath. The stakes were high for the malpractice firm, all or nothing. The table in the courtroom told the story. On the plaintiff side there were three seasoned attorneys and behind them, two legal assistants. Their desk was stacked with legal files meticulously labeled with various colored tabs. Their client was the "perfect storm". She was young, attractive, and single. She was a professional actress and with a facial deformity for the world to see.

Clearly, the medical malpractice firm invested a large sum of money preparing for this case. This included the cost for professional film recording, editing, and producing the movie documentation as well as obtaining four expert witnesses. It was a case of mismatch; the attorneys representing the plaintiff were more experienced and possessed greater expertise than the opposing lawyer.

Discredit the Expert

A professor and chairman of a mid-western university department of ENT testified against a private practice ear surgeon. The professor was well known as a head and neck cancer specialist. The plaintiff was an attractive, young, recently married woman who now was deformed by a grotesque facial paralysis. Following stapes surgery for otosclerosis, she woke up with facial paralysis. The plaintiff claimed that the ear surgeon was negligent and failed to meet the standard of care. This contention was supported by the testimony of the Professor of Head and Neck surgery.

The insurance companies have actuaries who are able to calculate cost benefit ratios and figure out the cost of trial verses the potential payout. This case seemed to be a "slam dunk" for the plaintiff and the insurance company was ready to settle without trial.

The doctor who was sued asked me to review the case. Initially, I agreed with the insurance company. No doubt, this case would be difficult to defend. When a young attractive women wakes up with a facial paralysis following surgery, this was a case of "res ipsa loquitur" or "the facts speak for themselves".

I tried to find a way to defend the doctor. Clearly, there were extenuating circumstances. Otosclerosis is a disease that caused deafness and was correctable by surgery. It was more common in young women, ran in families, and was caused by bony fusion of the stapes; one of the middle ear bones. In the advanced form, the bony growth was extensive and formed a solid footplate. This situation required using a special micro-drill and was performed by the most experienced surgeon. Normally the facial nerve courses close to the surgical site but is protected by a thin layer of bone. In this case, the nerve was bare without a bone covering.

My review included studying the deposition of the plaintiff's witness and his comments on the video of the actual surgery taped by the accused. We got a huge break when I realized that the head and neck surgeon confused the right side for the left. This was our opportunity to discredit the plaintiff's expert witness who hadn't performed ear surgery since he was a resident.

The case went to trial. The jury seemed interested in my explanation of the disease process and microsurgical approach. They were impressed that the middle ear surgeon worked through a thimble sized funnel with tiny instruments in a field the size of a ten cent piece. Magnification and illumination were provided by a binocular microscope.

Upon questioning the plaintiff, the defense lawyer brought out the patient's preoperative motivation to have this surgery performed and her acceptance of the risks. She had two previously failed surgical procedures. The previous surgeons could not remove the heavy bone over growth (solid foot plate) and failed to improve her hearing. She hated wearing hearing aids as they stuck out of her ears and were the source of constant ridicule and embarrassment since she was in high school.

The patient's testimony and discrediting the expert for the plaintiff, was the major factor that led to a favorable decision for the ear surgeon. I learned from this case that a slam dunk doesn't guarantee how a jury will respond.

On several occasions, opposing attorneys attempted to discredit me as an expert witness.

"Doctor, is it true that you are the Director of the Shadyside Hospital Sinus Surgery Center?"

"Yes, that is correct."

"Is it also correct that you organized two dissection courses each year held at the Shadyside Hospital Sinus Surgery Center and one ski meeting each winter at the Westin Hotel in Vail, Colorado?"

"Yes sir, that is correct."

"Doctor, is it also correct that you organized and directed three international symposia held at the Historic William Penn Hotel located in downtown Pittsburgh PA attended by 500 doctors and an international renowned faculty?"

"Yes, that is correct."

"Doctor is it also correct that these courses are profitable and a substantial part of your income is generated by these courses?"

I intentionally hesitated, feigning that I was troubled by the last question. The opposing attorney was trying to intimidate me. He was insinuating that my motivation for organizing and running these educational events was for personal financial gain.

"Financial gain is certainly not the reason; rather, it is because I am an addict. I'm addicted to teaching. All profits are deposited in a teaching fund for future courses and the funds are administered by a board of university professors. I can assure you that not a penny belongs to me."

On another occasion, the opposing attorney representing the plaintiff tried to discredit me. The case involved a bad result following sinus surgery.

"Doctor, I would like you to describe the anatomical parts of this model. Please note that this is a reproduction of the inside of an adult nose and can be disassembled to show the lateral nasal wall, the site of the surgical mishap. "

I responded, "I am impressed that you chose this model. Two years ago, Jon Coulter, a medical artist, and I designed and constructed this model as a teaching aid for our patients and students."

Attorneys have been forewarned not to ask an open ended question without knowing the answer. The attorneys who used this ploy on me regretted that they asked that question.

Chapter 9

Family Doctor

"The doctor who treats himself has a fool for a patient."
William Osler

If doctors were surveyed, I believe most would prefer not to treat themselves or their family. However, it sure is convenient to have a doctor in the house for emergencies.

68)   Harpooned

December of 1970 was the time for our annual winter vacation. The May family, including my parents and my mom's sister, "Aunt Minnie", were on our way to New Orleans in our rented camping bus. It was a ten hour drive from St. Louis to New Orleans on US Highway 10. About 8 miles before reaching New Orleans we turned off 10 to refuel in Metairie, Louisiana. After we stretched our legs and allowed the kids to run around, we got back on our bus and continued our trip to New Orleans.

We were waiting for the traffic light to change to green and turn onto Highway 10. My dad was in the driver's seat and I was in the bucket seat on the passenger's side. Seat belts were not required in those days. The kids were in the back of the bus in their bunks playing games or working on their coloring books.

Behind the driver's section there was a fold down table for dining with seats for two on both sides of the table. Minnie sat facing the back of the bus. My wife, Ida Ann, sat alongside of my mom on the side of the table facing forward. Ida Ann sat on the window side and my mom sat on the aisle.

Suddenly, without warning, there was a loud crash, a thump and a moan. I turned around and saw my mom lying on the floor of the bus. My wife had fallen on top of my mom. I quickly shifted into emergency mode. It was the "war zone" drill. Ida Ann was unconscious; my mom was shaken but not hurt. Minnie took care of the children and I concentrated on the needs of my wife.

Ida Ann was literally harpooned. An 18 wheeler coming off Highway 10 had brake failure and struck a street sign driving the post through the side of our bus. The post penetrated the side wall of our camper where my wife had been sitting. The post stabbed into the flesh behind her left shoulder. She and my mom were propelled off their seat and driven to the floor away from where they were sitting. The post remained in place protruding through the hole torn in the side of our mobile home.

The first responders immobilized Ida Ann's neck and placed her on a stretcher. She was carried out and placed into the ambulance. I followed behind and climbed into the rescue vehicle to be at her side.

We were taken to the closest ER, Daughters of Charity Health Center, a catholic hospital staffed by nuns. It was the day before Christmas and I was told that most of the medical staff was away for the holiday.

My wife was beginning to regain consciousness. She kept repeating, "Where are the children? Are they alright?" I reassured her that they were all fine but as soon as I finished my words of comfort, my wife would repeat her concern for the children.

There were no doctors in the ER; it was up to me to take control. My wife's skin was warm and dry and had normal color. Her pulse was about 70, strong and regular. There were no signs of central neurological deficits and her level of consciousness was improving from arousable to coherent conversation. Clearly, she had a concussion but no evidence of a more severe intracranial injury. She was breathing without pain or effort. Her abdomen was soft and without tenderness.

Her vital signs were normal and stable based on several interval measurements. Blood was drawn for a base line hemoglobin and hematocrit; fluids were started; tetanus toxoid and antibiotics were administered.

After checking off the ABC's, airway, bleeding and circulation, all seemed well. Based upon my careful preliminary survey, her wound required first aid and her concussion observation.

I ordered a radiograph of her head, neck/chest, and abdomen. There was a radiologist reading film so I introduced myself and we quickly developed a collegial relationship. I helped him read a sinus series of a fellow who was in a bar fight. This was routine stuff for me. The radiologist was impressed with my analysis. When my wife's films became available, the radiologist read them with me. He confirmed my clinical evaluation, the head, neck/chest and abdomen appeared normal.

We were offered an emergency helicopter evacuation to Tulane University in New Orleans. This was not an option. I wanted to keep the family (five children, my parents and Aunt Minnie) together. I announced that I was a physician with experience managing trauma and there was no indication that my wife needed more than wound care and observation. The nurses at Daughters of Charity Health Center were more than capable to provide that service. The nuns were so appreciative of my praise and confidence that Ida Ann received special care including an hour back message twice a day.

The hospital administrator, also a nun, allowed me to care for Ida Ann in the OR. The wound was debrided, irrigated and a drain was placed. The wound was dressed and she was returned to her room. Three days later, Ida Ann was well enough to continue our journey to New Orleans. By the time we arrived back home in St. Louis ten days later, her wounds were healed and she recovered completely from her concussion.

There are times when the house doctor can handle things. The hard part is not treating one's family rather knowing one's limitations and when to refer.

69)   Returned from Heaven

Our daughter, Rachel, was a two year old toddler when she walked off the diving board into the deep end of the motel swimming pool. This near tragedy occurred in Sarasota, Florida. Relaxation for a few days in a sunny warm climate was a welcomed break from the cold blowing snow that was so common in Pittsburgh in January. There was a medical meeting in Sarasota, Florida so I combined this with a family vacation.

We rented a motel suite on the Gulf of Mexico. There were ten of us including my wife, my parents, and six kids. Rachel was the youngest and had just started walking. The children watched cartoons that were playing on the TV; my dad was reading the sports page and drinking coffee with the rest of the adults who were sitting around waiting for the love of my life to complete making a pancake breakfast.

I heard Ida Ann asked "Where is Rachel"? I thought to myself, she's ok, crawling around somewhere. Then there was a hysterical scream, "Rachel is on the bottom of the pool!"

The adrenalin kicked in and the automatic system took charge. A run, a plunge and a grasp of Rachel's white pull over sweater and I had her limp body lying on the side of the pool. After a cough and spurt of water from her mouth, little Rachel took a breath. I was confident that she would make a complete recovery. The rest of the day her color remained pale and she lay in her crib sapped of her energy. I reassured my wife there was no need to take Rachel to the hospital. She was kept warm, bundled in a blanket. The next day she was herself, playing, climbing and walking around. The door to the outside patio and pool was locked shut.

When Rachel was old enough, she would ask, "Daddy, what happened?"

I told Rachel, "God took you up to heaven, kissed you on your forehead and told you, Rachel I am sending you back because you have a special purpose."

Today, Rachel Weiser is the senior attorney and educational director at Shurat Ha Din - Israel Law Center. Shurat Ha Din is a civil rights organization and World-Wide leader in combating terror through lawsuits.

70)   <u>Ticks and my Mother-in-law</u>

I was blessed with the kindest, warmest and most loving mother-in-law, Grandmom Dorothy, or Mom as I called her. Her favorite pastime, in addition to a thousand other interests, was gardening.

She called me about most medical issues, especially when it involved the head and neck. "Mark, the doctor down here has me all upset. You know that I am a smoker. I have been hoarse and there is a lump on the right side of my neck. I am scheduled for a direct laryngoscopy and biopsy and possibly a modified neck dissection. Should I be concerned?" She asked. "Mom, before you do anything, please come here to Pittsburgh." I answered.

She was hoarse, she did have a lump in her neck and she did have a tick in her scalp as I suspected. Her vocal cords were slightly swollen but otherwise normal, no signs of cancer. The neck mass was soft and tender with multiple others on both sides of her neck.

The tick located in her scalp just above her right ear solved the riddle. I suspected this all along because Mom loves to garden; there are lots of ticks where she lives and they carry tick-borne diseases. The two most common are Lyme disease (LD) and Rocky Mountain Spotted Fever (RMSF). LD is carried by the deer tick and RMSF by the larger sized wood tick. LD is caused by a cork screw shaped bacterial organism, Borrelia Burgdorferi, while RMSF is due to Rickettsia Rickettsii.

Both disorders present with similar signs and symptoms and both are curable by removing the tick and an appropriate antibiotic. However, RMSF is more dangerous and if not treated promptly, may be fatal.

Even though I didn't learn about Lyme disease until 1975, well past the time that I graduated med school, I included the disease in my list of differential diagnostic possibilities shortly after it was reported in 1975. By this time in my career, I was an established expert in diagnosing and treating patients with facial palsy. Each year I was referred 200 new patients with facial palsy and now Lyme Disease was one of the known causes.

A useful tip from this case: The best way to remove a tick is to grasp it with a fine pointed forceps close to its attachment to the skin and gently pull until it lets go. Try not to squeeze the stomach contents back into the victim and, make note, a hot needle and oils don't work.

71)   <u>House of Horrors</u>

Montefiore Hospital of Pittsburgh, a 900 bed teaching hospital, is part of the University of Pittsburgh complex. The hospital was founded in 1908 and funded by a group of Jewish philanthropists. It provided kosher facilities for Jewish patients and a place where Jewish doctors could obtain hospital privileges. The hospital played a key role for training Jewish doctors at a time when they were not welcomed at non-Jewish facilities.

In 1954, Montefiore Hospital became affiliated with the University of Pittsburgh School of Medicine. The patients were admitted to Montefiore by their private doctor who turned the responsibility for their care over to the house staff. The official hospital policy allowed the residents to manage the patients with the help of interns and medical students. This was the place where the University of Pittsburgh medical students began their clinical experience.

In 1978, my aunt Elva was visiting us in Pittsburgh when she developed pneumonia and was admitted to Montefiore Hospital on the service of a pulmonary specialist. He was a student of Harold Israel, Professor of Pulmonary Medicine at Jefferson Medical College in Philadelphia.

Aunt Elva was married to Uncle Max, my dad's oldest brother. We all loved her very much. She was a terrific cook and baker. My older sister, Libby and I always looked forward to visiting her for Thanksgiving dinner. Aunt Elva prepared a banquet with everything from home made cranberry sauce to whipped cream topped pumpkin pie. Besides the pumpkin pie, her layered pudding cake was my favorite.

Aunt Elva had one flaw; she smoked high nicotine content Raleigh's unfiltered cigarettes. She would smoke three packs each day! Her small apartment in West Philadelphia had an acrid cigarette smell. There were always ashtrays lying around filled with cigarette butts. Our aunt had a deep masculine smoker's voice and coughed constantly.

After a fit of coughing, she took a deep breath, like someone who swam across the pool under water and when reaching the other side would gasp for air. Aunt Elva was small and fragile, appeared emaciated and poorly nourished.

We visited her twice a day while she was hospitalized. The admitting doctor was never encountered. Progress reports were provided by the intern or medical student. The reports were not favorable. Aunt Elva had an infection that did not respond to the antibiotics and her oxygen saturation based on arterial blood samples were dropping in spite of a nasal mask delivering

100 percent oxygen. Her color was ashen and her breathing was labored.

We were asked to leave the room while arterial blood was drawn. As a doctor on the teaching staff, they extended me the courtesy to observe. There were four of them present, three medical students and an intern. Aunt Elva began to scream, "They are killing me, please make them stop."

I discovered that this procedure of taking arterial blood required sticking a needle into the radial artery, a spot on the wrist where one can feel the patient's pulse. This procedure is painful and requires a small pinch of numbing medicine or Xylocaine injected into the site over the radial artery.

I asked, "Why not use some Xylocaine?" "That is not our routine." One answered me. "Why do you need to repeat this procedure every hour?" I continued asking. One of the medical students without thinking, told me, "We take turns every hour and it is my turn to get some practice."

In other words, they were using Aunt Elva as a live mannequin. I stood between Aunt Elva and these ghouls. In a quiet and controlled tone, I said, "The party is over." Then the resident walked in. "What is the problem here?" I told him, "You are torturing my aunt. You have converted a teaching hospital into a house of horrors. "

The next thing caught me by surprise. Two-armed security guards accompanied me out of the building. I couldn't reach the private admitting doctor. There was one way to save my aunt from torture but the risk of killing her in the process was real. I arranged for an ambulance to transfer Aunt Elva to Professor Harold Israel's service at Jefferson Hospital in Philadelphia. Israel made the diagnosis based on the history. Aunt Elva had E. Coli bacterial pneumonia. With appropriate treatment, Aunt Elva had a complete recovery and lived three more years. My reward for my bold move was pumpkin pie and a layered pudding cake made especially for me.

A teaching hospital is essential for new doctors to learn but patients have rights. More on this topic in the story: The First Time.

72)	Take off the Gloves

We were in the Army (see Chapter 4 Military Doctor) and my mother-in-law, Grandma Dorothy, was visiting. "Mark, Ida Ann has a lump in her neck, take her to a doctor." She told me.

I asked the general surgeon at Darnell Army Hospital to take a look. I don't recall his name but he was short and stocky with blond hair cut short in a military style. He just finished his surgical residency, same as I, and came in as part of the Berry

Plan. A needle biopsy was taken and read by Leon Barnes, a pathologist who was also a Berry Plan recruit. His diagnosis was a benign pleomorphic adenoma or mixed tumor involving the submandibular salivary gland; a saliva gland that sits just under the jaw between the neck and tongue. The tumor was as large as a walnut but most importantly it was not cancer.

It was 1967 and in one year I would be at Washington University, the leading center for Head and Neck Cancer Surgery. I called Doctor Ogura, my chief to be. I hoped he would say, bring your wife to St. Louis and he would take care of her. That's what I would have preferred. Ogura advised that the surgeon at Darnell Army Hospital should be able to remove the tumor.

I asked the surgeon, "Have you ever seen a case like this?" He was a southern boy and a man of few words, "Nope." Did you ever perform surgery to remove a mixed tumor or assist in such a procedure?" "Nope." He replied. Well, that is reassuring, I thought.

The night before the surgery, Ida Ann got the pre-op risk options and benefits routine.

The presenting surgeon always used the plural, "We will make an incision in your neck below your jaw. The tumor will be exposed and removed completely. We need you to understand that there are two nerves that course by or through the tumor. One is to your tongue that carries sensation and one that moves your lower lip. If either of those nerves are removed with the tumor, you will have a numb tongue, a paralyzed lower lip, or both. One other possibility is that we might have to remove your jaw bone and neck lymph nodes. If they are involved, they will be removed with the tumor. Do you have any questions?"

Ida Ann told me years after the surgery, how frightened she was and did not sleep the entire night before the surgery.

It was assumed that I would serve as first assistant. I scrubbed, gowned and gloved. Ida Ann was prepped and draped. I usually mark my intended incision line with a marking pen. The surgeon took hold of the knife and started to cut. It was not the way I would make the incision. The incision should be lower and in a natural skin line. I shared my concerns. The surgeon took off his gloves and walked out of the operating room.

"Hey, where are you going?" I called after him. "Decide who is the surgeon!" He retorted. "You are, please accept my apology."

An hour later the surgeon stepped into the waiting room. "The tumor is out and your wife is in the recovery room."

I don't remember ever seeing that surgeon again. Ida Ann recovered; the scar was barely noticeable, no neural deficits and no recurrences after 40 years of follow-up.

Was this luck, skill, divine intervention, or all three?

Leon Barnes, the pathologist who interpreted the needle biopsy, became an internationally recognized Head and Neck Pathologist. He authored hundreds of articles and several classic books on this subject. We met up again at the Eye and Ear Hospital at the University of Pittsburgh. Leon became Professor and Chairman of the Division of Head and Neck Pathology at both the Medical and Dental School. We renewed our friendship, participated in teaching conferences, and coauthored several journal articles.

73)   First Time

Rectal Exam

My mom's brother, Uncle Willie, was one of my biggest fans. He couldn't wait for the day that I became a third year med student. I called him on the phone, "Uncle Willie, do you want me to come to your house?" He lived directly across the street.

I was so excited. "Today I got my doctor's bag and Sphygmomanometer, a blood pressure machine. I can take your blood pressure."

We had a routine; Uncle Willie was waiting for me to return home from school every day with his sleeve rolled up to have me take his blood pressure. It was always the same and his pulse was always strong and regular. I became the expert in my class at taking blood pressure, thanks to my Uncle Willie.

The novelty of taking Willie's BP every day became boring and tedious. I didn't have the courage to tell my top supporter that there would be no more BP clinics. One day an idea occurred to me, an approach that worked like a charm.

"Uncle Willie, I have great news for you. We changed services and I need to practice a new skill."

He called me "Bruddah" a name given to me by our house keeper when my older sister Libby and I were not yet twelve. My name became Brother and Uncle Willie pronounced it "Bruddah".

"OK Bruddah, I am ready." Uncle Willie told me.

"Today we started proctology and we have to practice doing rectal exams." I explained.

That was the end of taking blood pressures and everything else until graduation day.

Unconscious

Our grandchildren frequently ask if I ever passed out. I tell them the stories of the three times that I did.

The first time was really embarrassing. I was with a group of premed students who were invited to spend a day at Hahnemann as part of our indoctrination. We were herded into an operating room observation area, an open balcony that accommodated about 20 visitors. It sort of hung over the operating room and gave a bird's eye view. This was my first time in an operating room. The room was quiet and still. No one spoke and hardly took a breath. We were contained in a sterile capsule. There was a distinct odor of ether. The silence was broken when a nurse entered the room and started scurrying about making preparations for the planned surgery. There was a pan next to the operating table containing a sterilizing solution. She walked over to the pan. To get a better view, I leaned over the brass railing. At that moment, the nurse dropped some instruments into the pan. "Clang!"

I regained consciousness in Hahnemann's Emergency room. I remember two heads wearing masks; one was reviving me with smelling salts while the other was mumbling something about welcome back.

"You fainted." They explained.

I was so embarrassed. Who would ever predict that I would become a surgeon!

The second time I passed out, I was a first year med student learning anatomy by dissecting a cadaver with Miller, Miller and Miller, my partners. I heard my name paged and hurried to the blood bank. I had blood type A+, common and frequently requested. Donors were paid 50 dollars a unit and I could donate once a month. Most of the med students were married and some with children. We depended on subsidies where ever available. We would give blood and then immediately return to the anatomy lab to continue dissecting.

My bottle was full: the nurse disconnected my line and advised that I hang around, have a glass of orange juice and then return to the cadaver lab. I always knew what was best. I jumped off the table on my way back to the lab. I took a few steps and my lights went out. The intern on duty in the emergency room had an intubation set and was ready to shove a tube into my throat. I sat up, "Whoa, Whoa, Whoa, hold on! I am OK." I woke up just in time.

The third time I fainted was from the sight of blood. This was the most embarrassing; it was my own. We used glass syringes and recycled needles, no disposables in those days. I was injecting local anesthetic when the syringe cracked in my hand. The nurse noted blood under my glove and insisted that the torn glove be replaced. I put out my hand and the nurse removed my glove. I noted that the web between my thumb and first finger had a deep gash with blood flowing down my arm. It was my blood. I regained consciousness in the doctor's lounge and was told that a colleague completed the surgery.

Nasogastric Tube

There are procedures that seem simple enough until one is on the front line and has to do it for the first time. A nasogastric (NG) tube insertion is one of those procedures that looks easy but can be beyond one's skill level. Today, there are designated experts called "Alimenticians", a fancy name for Nasogastric tube inserters.

In my day, it was the ENT man who was called for all tube insertions in the head and neck region. An elderly lady was stricken with a brain stem vascular event (stroke). She was fully conscious but unable to swallow. An NG feeding tube was appropriate to maintain her nutritional and medication requirements.

One side of the nose is usually more patent than the other due to the fact that a deviated septum is common. The proper procedure is to place an NG tube on the open side after the nasal mucosa is decongested and anesthetized. This is achieved with a cotton pledget with 2 percent Xylocaine and a decongestant. A small feeding tube is placed in ice to make it stiff. Once this is accomplished, the tube is slowly inserted while looking at the oropharynx viewed through the mouth. If the tube is in the midline, it is in the wrong place. It must be on the left side of the back of the pharynx. The esophagus (the tube that leads to the stomach) is on the left and the trachea (tube connected to the lungs) is in the middle. Once in place, contents are withdrawn from end of tube using a syringe. Dark gastric juice is a favorable sign. Instilled air causes gurgling, and vibrations heard and felt in the belly area. This confirms that the tube is in the correct place. A lateral bedside radiograph confirms the tube is in the stomach.

The inexperienced will depend on an anterior posterior picture. The tube may be in the stomach or chest. This view can't make that distinction. On a lateral view, proper placement is acheived if the tube is located posterior along the spine. When all these steps are taken the tube must be securely sutured to the nose, ideally with 2-0 silk.

The steps described above were carried out in response to a well meaning nurse's aide who called me at 4 am to replace a feeding tube that a disoriented patient pulled out.
At 5 am I climbed back into bed. At 5:30 my bedside phone awakened me from my deep sleep. It was the on-call intern.

"You killed her, she is dead. She drowned in her feedings." The intern said. "Slow down. What are you talking about!?" I asked. He responded, "The postmortem exam (autopsy) is first thing in the morning. We will see how you killed my patient."
Eddie Fisher was the chairman of the pathology department at Shadyside. I called him at 8 am.

"Hi Mark, the autopsy was completed. She had a massive brainstem stroke and died." He explained.
"Eddie, where was the tube?" I asked. "The autopsy report says she died from a massive brain stem stroke." He repeated.

The physician-surgeon reader will probably understand Doctor Fischer's response that did not mention the location of the tube to support or deny the on-call intern's curiosity; "Did the patient die from a misplaced feeding tube?"

Doctor Fischer understood that the location of the tube was important to no one other than a medical-malpractice attorney. Doctor Fischer reviewed my detailed notes documenting the efforts of an expert ENT specialist who took every effort to place and secure a feeding tube. No one can guarantee or expect that a feeding tube can't become displaced.

The Star Spangled Banner

A background on Professor Eddie Fisher is appropriate to appreciate his uniqueness . Once a week, I would march my crew of fellows, residents, the intern and medical students to the Pathology Department for an afternoon session with Eddie Fisher. He loved the attention and shined in the teaching environment. One of our residents would provide the history and preoperative findings. Then a pathology resident would read the pathology from a tissue slide viewed through his binocular microscope. The image was projected on a large monitor where Fisher would explain the basis for his final diagnosis.

Normally that would be the final word and the conference would end. Reviewing the pathology of all my surgical cases was a routine learned as a resident and followed throughout my career. Pathology was one of my strengths. There were times when I requested clarification and one time I even dared to challenge Fisher's diagnosis. He loved to banter with me and the house staff was delighted with our, at times, heated disputes. I performed exploratory surgery on a patient to find the cause of her slowly progressive facial palsy. The facial nerve was sampled at various places along its course. There was a soft discolored area along the facial nerve where it emerged from the stylomastoid foramen, a spot at the skull base. Fisher reported the lesion as a benign aberrant ectopic minor salivary gland. Fisher searched the literature to support his diagnosis. He found a number of papers that fit his description.

I challenged him, "Doctor Fisher, this lesion is behaving like a malignancy and should be diagnosed accordingly. You have taught us on multiple occasions that making a diagnosis strictly based on how it looks on a slide must be reconciled with how it is behaving in the patient. This tumor is a malignancy."

When we dueled, I referred to him as Doctor Fisher and he referred to me as Doctor May or just May.

"May, let me remind you that I am the pathologist who deals with tissues and you are the surgeon who deals with the patient. This lesion on the slide is a benign aberrant ectopic minor salivary gland. If you want to call it malignant, that's fine. As far as I am concerned, you can call it *The Star Spangled Banner*."

We all had a great laugh and another path conference ended on a high note.

Now the reader understands why I chose this story for <u>First Time</u> or perhaps one of a kind. Eddie Fisher was a class guy.

About the Author

I was born in Philadelphia, Pennsylvania in 1936, 82 years ago. My grandparents were immigrants to America around 1900 who escaped Jewish persecution of Eastern Europe and Russia. My parents graduated high school and I was the first among all of the relatives to go to college. I relate my struggle of becoming a doctor, overcoming dyslexia, earning higher grades, which were required for Jews to gain admission to Medical School, and facing problems encountered during my medical career pursuing the truth.

Over the years, I told our children stories of experiences as a premed student at Dickinson College, a medical student and intern at Hahnemann in Philadelphia, PA, a resident in General Surgery and ENT at MCV Richmond, VA and, as a US Military doctor at Darnell Hospital, Ft Hood, Killeen TX. The stories I told were about when I was a Head and Neck Cancer Surgery fellow and the five years as full time faculty member at Washington U in St Louis. Finally, the stories included occurred during 22 years while in private practice in Pittsburgh Pennsylvania.

December 1996, we retired and moved to the mountains of Colorado. In September of 2008 we settled in Israel with 5 of our 7 children and 19 of our 27 grandchildren.

Our grandchildren heard their grandfather's medical stories from their parents and requested that the stories be written down so they could read them.

There is no way a grandparent could refuse such a request.

They urged me to include the story about the patient that was revived from the dead, the needle and the brain tumor, my first time in the OR and the time I fainted at the sight of my own blood.

I wrote 73 stories; the best of the bunch. Some of the stories are humorous, heroic or harrowing but all are true. The stories will be of interest to a wide audience because the stories represent one man's idealism that was passed to his students and most importantly to his children.

295

2010. Biking in Israel on the beach along the coast.

The author retired as Clinical Professor at the U. of Pittsburgh in the department of ENT in 1996. His career was distinguished as a teacher and a writer of 250 published articles and 4 text books where he documented new observations and surgical procedures on the topic of Facial Nerve and Sinus Surgery.

Dr. May shares personal stories that occurred from early childhood until present describing events that have shaped his life over a period of 82 years. The stories are all true; some humorous, some informative, some historical and some with important morals worthy of sharing.

These stories, for the most part, were enabled and influenced by his partner of 58 years, who set high standards for truth and virtue based on Torah values.

He is grateful and forever appreciative to Ida Ann for her love and guidance.

Epilogue

I started writing down Doctor Stories at the request of our grandchildren. Along the way, friends & family were recruited for feedback. The response was unexpected; in every case favorable.

Our grandchildren wanted to know if I had ever fainted at the sight of blood. They were surprised that their grandfather, the surgeon, did in fact faint at the sight of blood; the time his hand was cut in the operating room and he realized the blood was his own.

There are stories of making bold decisions that determined the life or death of patients, some strangers, but at times, close family members as well; saving our daughter from drowning, performing emergency surgery on my wife on Christmas Eve in a hospital far from home, and diagnosing a potentially lethal infection, contracted by my mother-in-law.

Dyslexia, diagnosed in the third grade, plagued me throughout the years of formal education; I couldn't read or spell; language skills were always above my pay scale, an enigmatic challenge. I almost flunked English and would never have qualified for medical school but was saved by the story of the Alligator and Turtle Race. I could have been bounced out of medical school for practicing without a license or arrested for working in a cocaine clinic.

My experience as a medical expert testifying in the courtroom provided insights into the medical malpractice system. My stories explain why I regret ever participating in a system that, in my opinion, is neither fair nor just.

The stories are told in a chronologic order and portray the rare and unusual life of an idealistic young man who became a dedicated husband, father, surgeon and teacher. Along the way, managing to learn from the best role models; my parents, my lifetime partner, Ida Ann, my teachers and students. The patients were the real heroes in these doctor stories.

It is my wish that these true stories will inspire others to try their best to be the best they can be. This is a small effort to demonstrate accomplishing a life of "can do" should be everyone's goal.

Approbations

Dad, these stories gave me a serious chill! B'H for your dyslexia and ingenious brain/ability to teach and write and gifted surgical hands!!! I'm so proud to be your son!

-- **Micah May MD**

A remarkable mix of fantasy and reality. Wonderful read of travels thru the imagination of a young man who emulates his heroes and chases his success. I love what you have achieved and was pleased to share your persona on your way to your goals.

-- **Norman J Schatz M.D., Professor of Clinical Ophthalmology, University of Miami school of Medicine**

If you want to take a deep dive into the life story of one of the giants in Otolaryngology, read Dr. Mark May's "Doctor Stories." Complete with his fascinating path to medicine, surgery, and ear, nose and throat surgery, Doctor Stories is filled with medical phenomena, personal vignettes, and an insider's view of the operating room in ways you've never experienced. A thoroughly enjoyable, insightful read.

-- **Nina Shapiro, MD. Professor of Head and Neck Surgery,UCLA** and author of *HYPE: A Doctor's Guide to Medical Myths, Exaggerated Claims and Bad Advice: How to Tell What's Real and What's Not.*

This is a terrific collection of fascinating medical stories written by a master storyteller.

Dr May is a great teacher and readers of all types should find these stories enjoyable.

--**Dieter Hoffmann, Otolaryngologist/Head and Neck Surgeon , Northwest Kaiser Permanente,** *retired*

I truly enjoyed reading your book, Medical Stories Your spirited "gung ho" activism as a student/athlete at Central High and Dickinson College certainly continued as you gained wide recognition as an expert in facial nerve problems and endoscopic management of sinus disorders. It's amazing how you remembered with such clarity the names, dates, times and places where so many of the meaningful moments in "your journey" occurred. So many of your stories are filled with humor and wisdom, and some with familiarity stemming from our long term friendship and joint choice of ENT as a specialty, "where a diagnosis can be made with just a glance".

-- Robert Simons, MD Clinical Professor of Otolaryngology and Head and Neck Surgery, Voluntary, at the University of Miami

(Former Chair of the Division of Facial Plastic and Reconstructive Surgery at the University of Miami

Former President of the American Board of Facial Plastic and Reconstructive Surgery

Former President of the American Academy of Facial Plastic and Reconstructive Surgery.)

"I have read Dr May's volume "Doctor Stories". The book is a fascinating and eye-opening account of the life of a dedicated healer who evolves into a deep thinking student of the human psychological as well as medical condition. Dr May narrates beautifully the empathy, humor and real-life tragedy that accompanies a man of medicine throughout his career. At times I was reduced to tears and at others, guffawing with laughter at the machinations of the real-life drama of human strength, endurance, frailty and tragedy. I would recommend this book to anyone with a heart, to anyone with a soul and to anyone with a lust for life, that, thank Gd, people like Dr May have spent their lives trying to preserve"

--Rabbi Alter Tzvi Amdurer, Raanana Israel

Doctor Stories authored by my beloved and distinguished friend Dr. Mark May, is not merely a delightful, thoughtful, enlightening and informative volume, sharing a lifetime of outstanding and advanced medical achievement and practice, but also a mirror into the soul of a kind, considerate, compassionate and accomplished medical educator and practitioner, whose greatest delight was restoring a smile to a paralyzed human face. It was my distinct pleasure to know and observe Dr. May in a variety of life's experiences; personal, social, communal, religious and professional, and in all of them, his lifelong search for meaning and focus on integrity and human sensitivity, distinguished his life and career. In Doctor Stories we discover one of the finest ENT specialists achieving prominence and success in his chosen medical specialty, rooted not simply in science and its labs, but steeped in a deep spiritual yearning for God's world and His prize creation - the human being. In Doctor Stories, Mark May invites us in to discover how the greatest of doctors, can remain among the greatest men of God.

--Rabbi Eliyahu Safran, Brooklyn, NY

Mark May provides in *Doctor Stories* an inside, honest and often humorous account of the career of one of the world's leading Otolaryngologists, spanning his life from kindergarten to retirement. The stories provide insights into the historical changes that occurred during Dr. May's 4 decade career. Each story builds in chronological order on reflections that stood out and shaped Dr. May into the excellent clinician, teacher, and author he became. May reveals that his dyslexia turned out to be the driving force that caused him to provide obsessive photo documentation and medical illustration of all his teaching discoveries that made him stand out to this day as an educator. An excellent read for those who have wondered about how a doctor evolves and for those in the mood for a behind the scenes look at the training and practice of medicine.

-- Barry M Schaitkin, MD, Professor of Otolaryngology, Residency Program Director University of Pittsburgh

I enjoyed reading your chapters from the 'modern era'. It felt like I was right there with you. I love the way that you were able to tell a story in such a straightforward manner; no futzing around. Your use of descriptors was direct and to the point. You gave just enough details to allow the reader to paint a vivid visual image. I am sure that this book will be added to the library of anyone that 'has been there'!

-- Eric Milch DDS, Oro-maxillo-facial Surgeon, Jerusalem, Israel

"Doctor Stories" by Mark May, M.D., a gifted diagnostician and creative head and neck surgeon, now retired, is both gripping and humorous. Gripping because of the author's unfiltered honesty about his initial shortcomings and the drama of his struggle to overcome them. Gripping also because of the stakes for each of the patients he describes. Be prepared to be in the operating room, looking over the surgeon's shoulder. The seriousness is leavened by humor. The author artfully weaves in the risible humanity of his mentors, colleagues, patients, and himself. The book is addicting. The only cure is to consume it.

--Arthur Karlin, Ph.D., Higgins Professor of Biochemistry & Molecular Biophysics, Physiology and Cellular Biophysics, and Neurology - Columbia University, New York, New York

If only I had this prior to working with you in 1988. At last I have a complete picture of what makes you tick. I found the stories compelling, and at times, self- effacing. I am glad that you included the medico-legal aspect of your journey, which will broaden your target audience. The short story format enables the reader to dip in and out, which will appeal to the time poor. Congratulations on compiling a memoire of your professional life. I wish you well in its publication.

-- Glen R. Croxson MD, Clinical Associate Professor, ENT, Sydney University, MB,BS (hons), FRACS

<u>Appreciation</u>

This book could not have been completed without the help of my dear family, friends and colleagues. Thank you to **Rabbi Alter Tzvi Amdurer, Francine Butler, Glen R. Croxson, Arthur Karlin, Micah May, Eric Milch, Larry Moses, Lee Rosky, Rabbi Eliyahu Safran, Barry M. Schaitkin**, Norman J. Schatz, **Adam Shapiro, Nina Shapiro, Robert Simons** and so many more!

A special thanks to my editor, neighbor, and friend **Pnina Jacobi-Yahid** for all her insight, advice and help.

Made in the USA
Middletown, DE
14 July 2019